METAPHOR
AND
MEANING

WELLER EMBLER

Foreword by S. I. Hayakawa

EVERETT / EDWARDS, inc.
DeLand, Florida

First Printing September 1966
LCCCN 66-25836

PN
228
·M4E5
C·l

Cover Design by Bill Brinkworth

Manufactured in the United States of America
by Convention Press, Inc., Jacksonville, Florida

For

KATHERINE

METAPHOR

AND

MEANING

ACKNOWLEDGMENTS

Thanks are due the International Society for General Semantics for permission to use articles which first appeared in *ETC.: A Review of General Semantics.* Acknowledgment is also made with thanks to *Art Journal* in which "Symbols in Literature and Art" was first published and to Teachers College *Record* for "The Rhetoric of the Absurd." Several of the articles have been revised, especially the Introduction, parts of which first appeared in *ETC.: A Review of General Semantics* as "Metaphor and Social Belief." The final chapter is new.

For valuable advice and editorial help, I am greatly indebted to Dr. S. I. Hayakawa, editor of *ETC.: A Review of General Semantics,* to my colleague Professor Leo S. Kaplan of The Cooper Union, to Mr. Richard Langford of the Everett Edwards Press, to Dr. Maxine Greene, editor of Teachers College *Record.* I wish also to thank the Trustees of The Cooper Union for a sabbatical leave of absence which gave me time to write some of these essays. I am glad to be able to express here my gratitude to Margaret and Marion Whaley for the happy environment of Hickory Hill Farm in the fall of 1964, and to thank Mrs. Elizabeth Ames for a richly rewarding visit at Yaddo in the last two months of 1964.

WELLER EMBLER

The Cooper Union

1966

CONTENTS

Foreword by S. I. Hayakawa / i

Introduction / iv

Literature as Metaphor / 1

Design as Metaphor / 12

Metaphor in Everyday Speech / 27

Symbols in Literature and Art / 45

Five Metaphors from the Modern Repertory / 58

The Language of Criticism / 80

The Rhetoric of the Absurd / 95

Language and Truth / 117

Metaphor and Beyond / 133

Bibliographical Notes / 144

Index / 158

FOREWORD

No one has expanded and enriched the idea of metaphor as much as Weller Embler. In traditional rhetoric, metaphor has long been known as a "figure of speech" — an embellishment to literary discourse. So long as metaphors were so regarded — as merely the paper panties on one's lamb chop — they could be ignored. Some, in seeking a genetic explanation of metaphor, have looked upon it as a failing of the primitive and prelogical mind. Some few, notably Susanne Langer, have said that metaphor is the fundamental process by which language grows and adapts itself to the changing world. No one, to my knowledge, has taken the position so boldly expounded in this volume that metaphors are the very stuff with which human beings make sense of the universe — that philosophies of life, "the philosophy of an entire generation, indeed, even of an entire civilization [are] implicit in the metaphors of creative writers."

To Professor Embler, a metaphor is not only the single statement, "He was a lion in battle" (to quote the example in my dictionary). As he shows in his chapter on "Metaphor in Everyday Speech," metaphors are the principles of organization by means of which we sort our perceptions, make evaluations, and guide our purposes. We do not use metaphors so much as our metaphors use us. "Figurative language," Professor Embler writes, "is the home of many a deep-seated, unexamined belief or mental attitude." To examine closely what we say is to learn much about the operation of our minds.

Professor Embler's view of metaphor is especially helpful to us in understanding the arts. "The novel," he writes, "is metaphor reflecting aspects of the interior life of human beings. . . . *Heart of Darkness* is only incidentally a description of the Belgian Congo. Essentially it is . . . about our inner wantonness, faithlessness, emotional incoherence. . . . It is also about the lonely light of reason which hopefully

i

and without ceasing would hold the jungle back." In his chapter on "Five Metaphors from the Modern Repertory," he demonstrates the many ways in which fiction, in Fitzgerald or Kafka or Gertrude Stein or Eugene O'Neill, expresses the inner life of our times.

Equally perceptive are Professor Embler's comments on art. "Design invariably," he writes, "from the simplest to the most complex, has meaning. Design is metaphorical, just as langauge is metaphorical. . . . Design is informed thought or emotion, an allegory of that which is within us." Armed with this perception and his luminous examples drawn from his wide acquaintance with modern art, I found myself recalling my own experiences with art and perceiving a flood of meanings that I had never understood so well before. It has also enlarged my understanding of primitive art to read that "without exception, each created article of culture is a figure of speech, a vehicle made to carry inner thoughts and feelings." I am sure that the reader will find Professor Embler's ideas as stimulating and enriching as I did.

Many years ago, before assuming his present position at the Cooper Union for the Advancement of Science and Art, Professor Embler was a pioneer in introducing semantics to undergraduate students at Syracuse University. Like other students of semantics, he finds the language of science and the language of art to be complementary, not opposed. Also, like other students of semantics, he believes that language must ultimately be connected with the things and events it stands for. As he says in his last chapter, there is a nonverbal "beyond" that metaphor points to.

In the present volume, Professor Embler proves himself a pioneer still, by explaining with clarity and distinction levels of meaning that other semanticists have yet explored but little.

S. I. Hayakawa

San Francisco State College

1966

INTRODUCTION

G RAMMARIANS have often studied to define what a metaphor
is. But it is more meaningful in our day to find out what a
metaphor *does*. The little words "like" and "as" exert an enormous
influence over our thoughts and our behavior; and there is vastly
more to figurative language than the customary pedagogical dis-
tinctions between similes and metaphors. Our behavior is a function of the words we use. More often than not, our thoughts
do not select the words we use; instead, words determine the
thoughts we have. We can say with some assurance that language develops out of social conditions and in turn influences
social behavior.

Modern rhetorics insist that written and spoken English
should avoid the hackneyed figure of speech. Triteness, they say,
is "evidence of a failure to attain animation and originality in
expression." But the trite figure is worn-out not because it has
been used often before, but because it cannot bear the burden of
new attitudes. Consider the following extended figure of speech
from the novel *Young Man with a Horn* by Dorothy Baker.

> Fortune, in its workings, has something in common with a slot-
> machine. There are those who can bait it forever and never get
> more than an odd assortment of lemons for their pains; but once in
> a while there will come a man for whom all the grooves will line
> up, and when that happens there's no end to the showering down.

Fortune (or the more common "Fate") is a concept for
which the only referent in the external world is a series of ob-
servable events without an assignable cause, and creative writers
in all ages have sought analogies which will force the concept of
fate, for the time being, at least, to accept a local habitation and
a name. For instance, to the Elizabethans, it was quite unbeliev-
able that the capricious order of happenings should be governed
by malicious creatures who looked like very old women. When

iv

the fantastical Witches appear before Macbeth and Banquo announcing Macbeth's ascendancy from Glamis to Cawdor to King, it appeared to Shakespeare's audience that the course of Macbeth's life was chargeable to the whims of the horrid sisters. What is important is not the originality of the metaphors "invented" by Dorothy Baker and William Shakespeare but the relationship which their figures of speech bear to their times. If we think of events of our lives as controlled by witches or even controlled by some force known only to witches, we shall behave in one way; if we think that the course of our experience is a matter of statistical probabilities, we shall behave in quite another way.

A whole philosophy of life is often implicit in the metaphors of creative writers, the philosophy of an entire generation, indeed, even of an entire civilization. In the great tradition of the western world, it has been common to liken (in some essential respects) men to gods. Classical man so loved the gods he had created that he wished to be like them. Ulysses was not a god, but he had many things in common with the classical divinities, and it was fair to call him god-like. In other words, it was important to the social attitudes of Homer's Greece to believe that some men at least were "like" gods; and it is common knowledge that this belief in the divinity of man was responsible for much that was fairest and best in the classical civilization. The statues of Phidias are metaphors inspired by this ideal; the temples and the great dramas and the noble philosophies all testify to the comparison.

By way of contrast to the Greek, consider the figurative language of a modern novelist. In one of John Steinbeck's short stories, "The Leader of the People," the old grandfather of the story had at one time been a man of the frontier world of Indians and buffalo. But it wasn't Indians that were important, he tells his grandson, Jody, "nor adventures, nor even getting out here. It was a whole bunch of people made into one big crawling beast. . . . Every man wanted something for himself, but the big beast that was all of them wanted only westering." While Jody thinks of "the wide plains and of the wagons moving across like centipedes," his grandfather continues, saying, "We carried life out here and set it down the way those ants carry eggs. And I was the leader."

We must remember that Steinbeck matured as a writer during the depression era and that his social philosophy grew out of the social problems of the 1930s. In his search for a social philosophy which could meet the problems of his day, he turned for assistance to the biological sciences. In these he found sound method, tested hypotheses, and, if it could be translated into language descriptive of human behavior, a body of usable information about subhuman life. Steinbeck was one of the first American novelists to think consistently and seriously, but not always clearly, and mostly with a political purpose in mind, of men as something other than men. And it became Steinbeck's habit to compare human beings with marine animals, with land animals, and with insects. It may be fairly said that Steinbeck's dramatic similarities between mice and men, between fish and men (*Sea of Cortez*), between centipedes and men, whether drawn from observation or embedded within the firm system of ecology, have changed the social thinking of many readers.

To future generations, an age may be known by the metaphors it chose to express its ideals. Between 1798 and 1859 a good deal happened to change men's minds about the world they lived in. Among other revolutions in thought not the least effective was the change in attitude toward nature. Wordsworth had said that nature was full of consolation, of joy, and of wisdom. Presently, however, as a result of geological and biological investigations, nature ceased to be regarded as "Wordsworthian" and came to be thought of as "Darwinian." The theory of natural selection brought about a new attitude toward nature that had perforce to be expressed and communicated in new figures of speech. Tennyson was not striving to attain animation and originality in expression when he described nature as "red in tooth and claw." The association of nature with tigers was striking, but for the Victorians it was also to become "true."

But it is here that we observe an important linguistic and social phenomenon. It will be noted that Homer does not say that men *are* gods but only that in certain respects they resemble gods. Wordsworth does not say that nature *is* a teacher, but only that nature is like a teacher. Yet when metaphor is new, those who find their attitudes implicit in the metaphor construe the metaphor to be a statement of identity, that is, a statement of fact. Figures of speech, when they are fitting and felicitous, and especially when they occur in print, give poetic sanction, as it were, to hitherto dimly felt, inarticulated beliefs. When metaphor is new, and when the reader does not enjoy the perspective vouchsafed by time, the metaphor is taken literally, and its function is not that of rhetorical device, but of statement of fact, *prescribing* certain kinds of behavior.

Iago is a villain, but a clever one, and he says many things which were pleasing to an Elizabethan ear. For instance:

> 'Tis in ourselves that we are thus or thus. Our bodies are our gardens, to which our wills are gardeners; so that if we will plant nettles, or sow lettuce, set hyssop and weed up thyme, supply it with one gender of herbs, or district it with many, either to have it sterile with idleness, or manured with industry, why, the power and corrigible authority of this lies in our wills.

We may find Shakespeare's figure entertainingly turned, and we may even agree with the sentiment expressed, but in the twentieth century we shall hardly be aware of more than a casual similarity between ourselves and gardens. But when my friend explains to me that life is like a pin-ball machine — that we are little balls shot out through an alley, kicked around from place to place, sometimes ringing a bell or flashing a light, and eventually falling into a trough and rolling out of sight — when he says this, I inquire whether his figure is not perhaps the perfect analogy. His figure has a lively meaning for us today because we believe in the laws of probability and half suspect the aimlessness of our existence. For all practical purposes, I am well prepared to think of life and pin-ball machines as identities, of taking my friend's metaphor as a statement of fact about human experience.

When we read in Friedrich von Schelling that "architecture is frozen music," we are charmed with the originality and neatness of the analogy. But when James Johnson Sweeney, in describing Piet Mondrian's painting *Victory Boogie-Woogie*, says that "The eye is led from one group of color notes to another at varying speeds; at the same time contrasted with this endless change in the minor motives we have a constant repetition of the right angle theme like a persistent bass chord sounding through a sprinkle of running arpeggios and grace notes from the treble," we are convinced for the moment that the canvas *is* music.

The figure of Socrates as a gadfly is interesting but seldom taken literally. Yet when the villain in the movies is called a "rat" and shot thrice in the abdomen forthwith, it is a nice question whether the villain was a man or a rat. We know that Grieg's music is not pink bonbons stuffed with snow, although we rather admire the aptness of the similarity and the sensuousness of the image. Yet when someone says of the music of Shostakovich that it is the "cacophonous scream of a communist manifesto," we wonder if that is not perhaps "true." We are delighted with the little girl who said that carbonated water tastes "like my foot's asleep," but when we say a dish we don't like is "garbage," it is indeed! When Byron says of poetry that it is the lava of the imagination which prevents an eruption, the metaphor strikes us as an amusing romantic definition of poetry; but when a contemporary writer (I have forgotten who) says that a poem is the sublimation of the irritant that troubled the poet, just as a pearl is the "higher order" of the grain of sand that irritated the oyster, we accept the metaphor as a statement of fact about all poetry.

One further example will suffice to illustrate how meaning (and hence knowledge) is dependent on the figures of speech we use when we talk about something. Theories of communication are at the moment of commanding importance in many — one might almost say all — branches of thought. (It has even been suggested that we are suffering from over-communication.) However that may be, the metaphors of communication theory are revealing of the way we indentify the human nervous system with the devices of modern technology. Forty years ago, as I remember, lecturers in psychology spoke of "neural patterns," and listeners visualized intricate networks of roadways (highways, byways, paths), some, like the roads in Robert Frost's poem, wide and well-traveled (the old thoughts and reflexes), and some less well-traveled and wanting wear (new thoughts and delayed reactions). A generation later, the nervous system was likened to a complex telephonic organization in which messages are sent out through central exchanges over the "wires" of the system to all areas of the organism. Recently, the telephone metaphor has been supplanted by an electronic metaphor in a theory of efficiency called cybernetics, in which the human nervous system is identified with life-imitating automatic machines controlled by electronic devices with their own "feedback," in which, says Norbert Wiener in his book *The Human Use of Human Beings*, "past experience is used not only to regulate specific movements, but also whole policies of behavior. Such a policy-feedback may, and often does, appear to be what we know under one aspect as a conditioned reflex, and under another as learning." Today, as a complex of routes or wires conveying messages, the nervous system is all but abolished in favor of bio-chemical energy exchanges.

What the human brain, or mind, or nervous system will be likened to a century from now is unpredictable. New analogies will depend on future social and neurological theories and on future social and technological developments. In any case, it appears that cultural beliefs and ideals are deeply embedded in the figurative language we use to describe the human condition. In imaginative literature, with which most of the essays in this book have to do, in everyday speech, in social thought, in the representational aspects of the fine arts the meaning is, more often than not, in the metaphor.

Literature as Metaphor

FROM THE ILIAD to the latest murder mystery, nearly any work of fiction may be studied as an extended figure of speech, giving us understanding of our inner life by narrating outer events. If we may make the distinction at all, our inner life—our feelings and affections, our thoughts and beliefs—exists more positively for us and is more present to us than our outer life. But as we know from constant experience of the inadequacy of language, our inner life is impossible of precise articulation. "If we could only tell how it is with us," we often say, "everyone would understand." But others can never know directly our inner life. Hence we have invented an indirect way of talking about the inner self—through fiction, painting, music—through all the arts. The artist says, Let my work serve as my advocate with the world, or, as Emily Dickinson said, as my letter to the world.

The novel may be said to describe our inner life in terms of what happens outside ourselves. The events in a novel are not "true"; they do not constitute life. Instead, they are a highly abstract substitute for life. But given sequence and form, they show forth and make manifest the inner life. Joseph Conrad's novel *Heart of Darkness* may be thought of as an extended figure of speech used to illuminate the passions and the life within. Conrad presents the reader with outer events which may be said to be *like* inner events. On the surface, *Heart of Darkness* is a story about Marlow, the narrator, and Kurtz, the protagonist. But below the conventional event level, the novel is metaphor reflecting aspects of the interior life of human beings, reflecting not the heart of darkest Africa, but the most secret depths of the human heart. And that is why we can read *Heart of Darkness* and understand it though we have never been on the banks of the Congo nor have taken part in the experiences which happen there to Marlow and Kurtz.

Kurtz is a complicated personality. He possesses great personal magnetism, a compelling voice and manner, a deep Christian faith. But in the jungle (which very obviously does not have to be an African place) he is reduced by his passions and his surroundings to a savage madness, taking part in unspeakable primitive rites. Conrad does not say what these mysteries consist of (though head-hunting is clearly one). But it is the interior "horror," the abysms to which the inner life itself can fall, that he writes of in the wild dances by the river's side, the corrosion of greed and of pride, the desolation of spirit consumed by the insane illusion that mortal man can be God.

Against this wilderness of moral evil, Conrad has placed Marlow, who also represents the inner life—the serene, detached inner life. Conrad presents Marlow to our understanding as the symbol of that inner clarity and order which strives to keep the jungle back, the inner jungle as well as the outer jungle. In Marlow we see the exercise of reason and of moral lucidity. *Heart of Darkness* is only incidentally a description of the Belgian Congo. Essentially it is about the grief of savages and of white men, about our inner wantonness, faithlessness, emotional incoherence, and the vague ruthless indifference that seems to be a part of nature but is really a part of ourselves. It is also about the lonely light of reason which hopefully and without ceasing would keep the jungle back.

All overt acts may be thought of as metaphor expressing an inner condition, so that the outward act is only a function of an inner need. And the needs of the inner life are all, finally, that we are concerned with. Even the senses are useful only to satisfy an inner command. So it is that hate or anxiety or love or shame or experience of the beautiful are inner states. They do not exist in nature outside ourselves. (We do not say that the wind hates or the sun loves, unless we are speaking metaphorically about ourselves.) One of the purposes of art is so to use outward behavior that it shall serve as metaphor to describe inner feelings.

Consider, for example, *Salome* by Oscar Wilde. *Salome*, for Oscar Wilde, was a drama about a martyr—John the Baptist. Wilde used a biblical incident as a figure of speech with which to describe his own position in Victorian society. The head of John is, metaphorically, Wilde's head, and it is brought in on a silver salver before London society by the sadistic and hypocritical Salomes of the late nineteenth century. *Like* John, Wilde is victimized by the powers of society. In the Freudian sense, one might say that by 1892 Oscar Wilde had already chosen to be the victim, and that in *Salome* he is writing about what might happen to him outwardly. But far more significant, by 1892 Wilde is writing about his own inner experience and his society's inner experience of moral victimization and sacrifice. Wilde must have seen himself as a voice crying in the wilderness against the hypocrisy, the vanity, the vulgarity of his age. John the Baptist is imprisoned; Wilde is imprisoned. John is slain as the victim by Salome, whose inner passions are such that she requires a victim; and Wilde is slain as a victim by a society whose inner passions are such that it requires a victim.

Aubrey Beardsley was quick to see the likeness between John the Baptist's martyrdom and his own precarious position in London society; and his illustrations for Wilde's *Salome* are among the best of his drawings, replete with every suggestion of sensuality, lust, cruelty, and base passions. But the immense irony lies in the fact that artists like Beardsley and Wilde thought of themselves as moralists, scolding and scorning the crude and the false which they saw everywhere around them. What enraged Beardsley, as what enraged John the Baptist, was that he was not taken seriously as a preacher and prophet, exorcising sin (or, as William Butler Yeats suggests in *Trembling of the Veil*, taking it upon himself) and ugliness that innocence and beauty might live.

The drama *Salome* is, then, a figure of speech describing the inner life and feelings of Oscar Wilde, and perhaps in addition of all the "decadents" of the *fin de siecle*. The feeling of victimization was acute in many young writers and artists in the late nineteenth century, and many were in one way or another, figuratively speaking, sacrificed to the good name which society intended, however hypocritically, to keep.

The ways of talking about human experience are manifold, perhaps infinite; and the creative thinker is he who refreshes the

3

life within by seeing new and telling likenesses between the inner and outer worlds. The artist uses the materials of experience to fashion an image of what is going on within himself, and what he creates is an allegory of his own soul. In addition, there seems to be at any given historical time a common reaction among creative thinkers to the cultural experiences of the age in which they live. The creative artist makes the world over in his own image, but he refers often to common thoughts and feelings.

The Impressionist poets and painters and composers of the late nineteenth century illustrate this notion. Where ugliness prevailed and the spirit languished, in a world where there was mostly noise and no music, where there were sights that offended, and where there was no end of words that said nothing, the Impressionists came to the rescue of the inner life by creating the world as a place of dreams, a world trembling in loveliness behind the veil, full of mystery and romance, and an enduring calm, as the fair and shining *appearance,* as Nietzsche says, of the Apollonian dream. Though they were not systematic in their Platonism, it was the spiritual life that they wished to encourage, and it was to Platonic idealism that they turned for inspiration. And they chose nature as material with which to allegorize the beauty and the peace that are within, if one will only call them forth.

Monet and Pissarro and Sisley and Debussy and Ravel and Mallarme tutor the spirit in terms of a nature that is composed and beautiful. They create shapes and effects which delight the inner eye and astonish us with moods and inspirations we had vaguely felt but never quite allowed to come to the surface. Oscar Wilde measured the success of the Impressionists when he said, "Life imitates Art far more than Art imitates Life." The Impressionist painter takes us through sun-lit villages and woods and hillside orchards to quiet groves dotted with sunlight and deep shadows, through delicate yellow gardens, past terraces of flowers warm and fragrant, to still ponds of milk-green lilies. And the boulevards too and the bridges and railroad stations, the house-lined lanes and cathedrals—how full of charm they suddenly become! The Impressionist articulates the opulence and generosity of the sun, caressing all it falls on with a sweet intimacy, making a world bountiful of sensuous delights, of invitations to contemplate the endless variety and richness of natural sights that speak of peace and well-being. But it is the fair and shining *appearance* of nature, not nature absolute. For the beauty is within, and nature has served only as the agent. The Impressionists excited the spirit to a new vision of loveliness, an inner life of "quiet breathing," *like* a composed and sun-lit garden.

Paradoxically, art mirrors not so much the outward aspects of a civilization as the inner life of man. Contemporary art and fiction make visible not so much our industrial world, our wars, towering cities, and fast movement, as they do the adventures of man's soul in an industrial world, on war fields, and in great cities. The Expressionist painters and composers give us a representation of inner frenzies, so common to the twentieth century everywhere, in objects and sounds that are wild and frantic. It is Van Gogh's inner life that we see represented in his tortured cypresses; and our own inner life responds to the visions of twisted rooms and trees and courtyards. Seldom do we see nature as he presents it to us; but our minds are often as coiled and contorted as his ambagious shapes. In the early Schonberg music, such as *Pierrot Lunaire* (1912), one listens to sounds that are a representation of the soul's crying. And Stravinsky's *L'Histoire du Soldat* (1918) is an allegory which uses a weary foot soldier returning home for his leave as a representation of the modern mind confused and misled by influences seemingly diabolical. Nor is Alban Berg's *Wozzeck* (1925) so much a story of a slow-witted, unhappy soldier and his beloved mistress as it is a metaphor of the misery of an inner life distressed beyond endurance by violence and treachery. In a self-portrait, Kokoschka points to his own breast to indicate that the painting is not about his outward appearance but rather about the turbulence, the bitterness, and the agitation within.

Among the most powerful of modern allegories are the stories and novels of Franz Kafka. *Metamorphosis* (1916) is reminiscent of the medieval beast fable, and though its moral is clothed in fantastic garb, it is nonetheless palpitatingly present. Ostensibly the story is about a young man who wakens one morning to find that he has been changed into a particularly revolting kind of insect. The story expresses the difficulty of communication between young Gregor Samsa and his family, the impossibility of telling them how it is with him, that he is not really monstrous and repulsive, that he has a kindly, sensitive nature, and that if they could only know him as he really is within, they would not look upon him as a loathsome creature. But he is scorned and shut away. Though we are not insects, we sometimes behave as though we were; and a modern way of describing our behavior and the behavior of others is by comparing ourselves with insects. Gregor Samsa strives to vindicate himself, but the great world of unreason outside him, capricious, inscrutable, inhuman, refuses to accept any rational explanation. Each of us knows that vindication for his behavior lies within himself, and that, curiously, his own explanation is wholly reasonable.

Surrealism as a movement in painting, music, fiction, and the cinema has had an enormous vogue since its beginnings in the second decade of the twentieth century; and surrealism employs the language of metaphor. The dream images of Giorgio de Chirico, the bizarre figures of Max Ernst, the strange Sabbath phantoms of Kurt Seligmann, the sea-floor creations of Ives Tanguy, and the paranoid spectacles of Salvador Dali are reflections of interior emotions whose home is in the dark night of long-forgotten primitive urges and drives, emanations from strange cabinets of the mind. These images are not representations of outward experience as we know it empirically in terms of cause and effect. The metaphors of surrealism are pictures of the inner psychic world, representations of dreams and waking fantasies, nightmare terrors and anxieties, metaphysical agonies, and unimaginable horrors—the soul's life in the twentieth century.

In a sense we think of everything as hidden: information, human motives, movements of the enemy. The truth about the physical universe is hidden. There is the hidden meaning of dreams, the hidden value of x, the hidden meaning of the poem. There is the search for hidden lands, for ancient ruins, for precious metals and precious stones, for material resources hidden in the earth. Indeed, even the search for God is not an uncommon endeavor. And perhaps the most devoted and anxious search of our time is the search for the energy of the atom; and we say that we seek "inside" the atom for its secrets, as we search inside our hearts for the secrets that are there. Salvador Dali's "The Slave Market with the Disappearing Bust of Voltaire" and Pavel Tchelitchew's painting entitled, appropriately, "Hide and Seek" are examples of the use in modern painting of the double image and of the search for the hidden.

In order to show forth the hidden world of the irrational life, the surrealists produced, according to Andre Breton, "a crisis of the object," and it is this crisis which makes for bizarre, incongruous arrangements that are *like* the delirium of the mind; their paintings are really allegories narrating the life of the mind in the twentieth century.

As one proceeds through the history of modern creative work, it becomes obvious that the artist is saying one thing in the guise of another, that he does not, indeed cannot, speak directly of the life within. In *The Waste Land* (1922), T. S. Eliot speaks of our spiritual impotence, using the analogy of the mythical Fisher King, whose wounds cannot be healed by the ineffectual, wayward modern deliverer; this same impotence of spirit is found in Hemingway's *The Sun Also Rises* (1926), using the parallel of the emasculated hero (the fisher king) and the unbridled lust of the heroine. In their different ways of presenting the outward story, this metaphor of impotence is found in D. H. Lawrence's *Lady Chatterley's Lover* (1928) and William Faulkner's *Sanctuary* (1931). Other themes in modern literature make use of such metaphors as the bridge in the poetry of Hart Crane; the resurrection in the plays of William Saroyan; the "lost" in the novels and stories of F. Scott Fitzgerald; the grave and the wilderness in New England poets like Robert Frost and Edwin Arlington Robinson and in the paintings of Edward Hopper; the metaphor of "home" in Thomas Wolfe; the Orphic descent in Jean Cocteau and Stravinsky; the Hell metaphor in Sartre and in the revival of Dante studies of the twentieth century; the idyll in Sandburg and Steinbeck and Grant Wood; and in the figure of the "test" or "trial" in the theme of struggle of most popular fiction. The prevailing metaphor of modern fiction is the metaphor of violence, of the violence within embodied in overt acts of struggle and of flight.

Though our world of today is one of extreme violence, it is

7

not true that most people living the everyday routine lives of our society are either given to or are the subjects of violent acts. Though it would be absurd to deny the abundance of rape, murder, mayhem, manslaughter, suicide, torture, assault, arson, enslavement everyday everywhere, still, considering the density of modern society, there is not as much actual overt violence as one would suppose from the evidence of motion pictures, television, comic books, radio, and cheap fiction. On the other hand there is universal inner violence, fear, and treachery. It is the great inner conflicts and tensions that modern story-telling describes; and it is the translation of fiction's outward beatings, stranglings, stabbings, and shootings into our own inner struggles that we make when we read or watch or listen.

Since the tempest within will not submit to description in words of exact reference, the tempest without must serve as metaphor to tell about the soul's life. Modern fiction has chosen the device of *hyperbole* with which to show forth the inner life— all the shocks the spirit's heir to in our time—the insults, the humiliation, the sacrifice, the moral corrosion. For the most part, the modern story-teller chooses to deal with the extraordinary incident. Being more dramatic, it is more immediately understandable, reflects more directly the conflicts of everyday life. The violence and the fear of violence that is in us and so much a part of our psychological life are amplified many times in the metaphor of melodrama. The terror of the cinema screen and the ferocity of, for example, *Sanctuary* are mirrors held up to the terror and rage of our inner lives. Thus, the age of anxiety gives away its inner tensions in the works of popular writers like Graham Greene, James M. Cain, Dashiel Hammett, Mickey Spillane; in the cartoons of Charles Addams; in the plays of Tennessee Williams and Arthur Miller; in the operas of Carlo Menotti; in the films of Alfred Hitchcock, Billy Wilder, Raoul Walsh, Carol Reed, and Roberto Rossellini. Not that violent death does not occur in daily life; still it occurs but seldom to the 13,000,000 people who read the fiction of Mickey Spillane. Modern novels and motion pictures express our fears, our desires, our anxieties, our hate, all that troubles inwardly—frustration, fear of poverty, of spinsterhood, of losing status, of loneliness,

8

discrimination, humiliation, shame, heartache, of being sacrificed, of slavery, and of tyranny.

One of the main themes of T. S. Eliot's play *The Cocktail Party* is the theme of sacrifice, and Eliot uses the device of hyperbole to reflect and magnify the life within. Celia Coplestone, hurt by love, finding her life empty, grows to a deep awareness of sin and feels that she must atone, not for anything specific, but for the sinful everywhere. At the advice of Reilly, the psychiatrist-priest, she joins an order as a nurse and goes to the Far East, to a place called Kinkanja, where she works with two other Sisters in a Christian village. In the last act of the play we learn that while she was in Kinkanja an insurrection broke out among the heathen, and that she was taken captive, and crucified near an ant-hill. Now clearly Eliot is not telling his story for the purpose of shocking his audience with an instance of extreme violence. But by using the incident, he is able to express that inner sacrifice each of us is forced to make daily. For it is in Celia's giving herself away that the others in the play can live with greater awareness of themselves. Sacrifice is one of the main themes of western literature and appears often in modern works, not because of the researches of Sir James Frazer, but because sacrifice is an eternal part of all human experience, especially among aggressive peoples, where many are sacrificed to the importunities of success or failure, and to the vicissitudes of much and little.

In Hemingway's short story "The Killers," the story plot interests the reader to be sure, but the calculated murder of a defenseless man by two gangsters is only a framework with which to tell about the calculated intellectual and emotional, moral and spiritual murder that we commit and undergo daily. The black-coated, kid-gloved figures move with the assurance of destiny toward the cowering, abject mortal who must await his doom with such resignation as he can muster. Our inner fears are reflected in these great outer fears, our "waiting" is reflected in the agony of Ole Anderson. These black-coated ministers of evil are symbolic of the doom that seems to hang over the twentieth century; they are the nameless fears that one waits for with his face turned to the wall. They are insecurity and anxiety, moving with sublime indifference, the embodiment of all the

9

murderers of the spiritual and moral life. In "The Killers" we see all the violence and malice in the world suddenly concentrated on one human being, a visual image of our innermost fears.

One of the most violent of modern novels is Faulkner's *Sanctuary*. Very nearly every known crime is committed in its pages, with unflinching, graphic description of the details. And the novel is memorable for this reason. But its importance lies in the analogy it presents of the spiritual and moral life, of the life within—of greed, sacrifice, blind hate, agony, moral indifference, injustice, lust, brutishness, fear, impotence. The unnatural rape may have occurred in, as we say, real life; but the inner life is torn and mangled a thousand times to one overt violation of our persons. The inner humiliation, the shame, the enslavement—all these we experience many times over. And in the lynching, vicious enough and real, Faulkner presents, hyperbolically, an allegory of the spirit consumed in little daily lynch fires. What is this iron string Popeye but the taut rage of the world?

The following concluding paragraphs may be considered a kind of recapitulation of the main theme of this essay in terms of a rather extended analysis of *Death of a Salesman,* by Arthur Miller.

It is not strange that *Death of a Salesman* as play and as motion picture should have been emotionally stirring to many people. Although our most popular literature is still the "success story," failure is by no means unusual in our society. On the contrary, it is very nearly universal. If the chief psychological personality of our time is he who must be impressive, must draw attention, whose fantasies are those of power over others, and who must be "big" at all costs, then it is obvious how far we all come short of the promised heights. Our culture makes urgent an intense and passionate self-concern. Where there is so much of everything, and where our megalomania urges us on to have more and more, anything less than the most is ruin. In a highly competitive society where status is evaluated in terms of power and goods, each item of lack is irreparable loss. Where one wants everything, one cannot possibly succeed. It is not astonishing then that very nearly everyone should feel within him that he is a failure, that he has not achieved really to any of the many possibilities of glory, and that in the eyes of his fellowmen his life has miscarried pitiably. Not that we admit to others our feeling of inferiority, of insecurity, of failure; but in the generations coming to maturity between George Babbitt in 1922 and Willy Loman in 1949 many men in their middle years have tortured themselves with the belief that they were shameful and disgraceful failures.

Critics of *Death of a Salesman* were quick to note that Willy Loman had put his trust in the wrong social values and that his false ideals were his undoing. It is true that the importance of Arthur Miller's play lies in its veracity as a social document and in the moral that adorns the story. But it is not so much that *Death of a Salesman* warns against false values as that it tells all our unspoken fears of being wrecked and cast away on the scrap-heap of the twentieth century. Many have flourished with just such ideals as poor Willy had. Whether rich or poor, of good or ill repute, many people still believe deeply in the values that brought Willy Loman to an untimely end. But these people are not disabused of their illusions as he was.

Death of a Salesman is a morality play, and Willy Loman stands for those who commit suicide out of disillusion and for those who come only just short of taking their own lives. Like all great worldly failures, Willy knew the violence of disenchantment. Lover of illusion, when he was disillusioned, he could not bear it. It is crushing to learn that success is relative and temporary. It is tragic to learn that worldly failure is absolute. To win is to win, really, very little, as the world goes; but (as the world goes) to lose is always to lose everything. In the midst of ruin, one learns that each day of his life, nay, each hour, he has failed somewhere. Who is he who has the temerity to boast of success when every moment has yielded a harvest of errors and regrets and vanities. Like our faults, our most egregious failures are unknown to us, but they are there waiting like an infection for the moment of weakness, when the props of self-delusion are knocked away. Willy despairs when he learns that failure has always been imminent and has at last arrived.

Death of a Salesman is not about the worldly failure of one human being; it is about the universal spiritual failure of our time.

11

Design as Metaphor

BEFORE ME is a reproduction of a painting by Giorgio de Chirico. What does it mean, this weird picture called *Il Trovatore*, and why on earth should anyone have chosen to paint such a picture? The main figure in the painting suggests a man, but its feet are cloven hoofs, its legs and thighs are like the lower appendages of a puppet, joined loosely together, and smoothly shaped out of painted wood. Its torso is a medley of triangles in dark greens, browns, and yellows, a grotesque arrangement of shapes, odds and ends from under the carpentry bench. The figure, like the Venus of Milo, is armless. Its melancholy head is the shape of a football, or an egg, and appears to be stitched down the center and tied round the middle in a bow of black ribbon. The head reminds one of those chickenwire forms used to display millinery in shop windows. The whole mannequin, strange and sad, is supported by wooden braces (for it is not so well balanced as the Venus) and is set off against a background of enigmatic spaces with dusky shadows, against an architectural motive with ominous doors and windows that watch the empty scene intently, and against, in the distance, forbidding bottle-green skies. On the left there falls a mysterious shadow across the piazza floor of the scene, the shadow of a human figure, a stranger, silent, inquiring, reproachful.

It would be difficult to say what this painting "means," though it must stand for something the artist felt or had in mind. The modern artist may seem often not to have premeditated the content or design of his painting, yet his art is not whimsical or casual. He is serious and intends that his art shall be meaningful. What is more, his art invariably has some kind of emotional impact on the observer, though the emotion may not be readily articulated in words or be the same emotion that inspired the painter. What *Il Trovatore* means to me may not be in one-to-one correspondence with what it meant to the painter when he was making his picture. Indeed, the iconography may be, probably was, intensely personal to the painter. But the painting hangs on my wall and "stands for" thoughts and feelings of today. The painting is part of my environment and says something to me that I can translate into words.

The mannequin is clearly a troubadour, for that is the title of the picture. Here lies obvious irony, that this weak fantastic patched-up creature should be said to represent the twelfth-century heroic lover, debonair maker and singer of love songs. The figure is no Manrico, nursed and reared by gypsies, duellist, romantic knight. This dreaming puppet is the modern troubadour, ineffectual, with geometry for a heart, but, curiously, like Manrico, a being capable of suffering, and, if not a tragic hero, at least a tragic personality.

Why is the Chirico puppet supported by braces? And what are these braces that keep the figure standing upright? There comes to my mind a sonnet by Matthew Arnold, which is in a way a considerable comment on the painting.

> Who prop, thou ask'st, in these bad days, my mind?
> How much, the old man, who, clearest-soul'd of men,
> Saw The Wide Prospect, and the Asian Fen,
> And Tmolus' hill, and Smyrna's bay, though blind.
> Much he, whose friendship I not long since won,
> That halting slave, who in Nicopolis
> Taught Arrian, when Vespasian's brutal son
> Clear'd Rome of what most sham'd him. But be his
> My special thanks, whose even-balanc'd soul,
> From first youth tested up to extreme old age,
> Business could not make dull, nor Passion wild:
> Who saw life steadily, and saw it whole:
> The mellow glory of the Attic stage;
> Singer of sweet Colonus, and its child.

Ours, if one were to judge only from what has been said about them, are "bad days." And one might well ask whom he can turn to for intellectual and spiritual support in these parlous times. First, says Arnold, Homer, because he was clear-souled. But there is, alas, no Homer in the painting. Nor is there an Epictetus, "halting slave," unless the figure itself is a forlorn stoic, perhaps very much more slave than philosopher. And Chirico might well have claimed both Homer and Epictetus as countrymen, for he was himself both Greek and Italian. And lastly there is Sophocles, who saw life steadily and saw it whole, as the puppet figure certainly does not. Chirico's mannequin sees life hardly at all, except as a riddle, a contemporary sphinx (the shadow in the painting?), who will not be answered and who claims her victims with monstrous indifference. What props our modern figure are the meaningless sticks of modern life, holding the miracle of man (though he sports vestiges of nobility in his blue cloak) by the nape of the neck.

When I look at *Il Trovatore*, my attention is called irresistibly to another poem, "The Hollow Men," by T. S. Eliot. Eliot's poem is dated 1925, and Chirico's picture is dated 1917. One may reasonably suspect that Eliot knew the painting, was even, conceivably, inspired by it, or by any one of the many Chirico paintings that show strange, puppet-like figures with the egg-shaped heads. These heads, are they filled with straw, fit only to display bonnets?

> The eyes are not here
> There are no eyes here

T. S. Eliot's poem is an illuminating companion to Chirico's painting. Modern man is frustrated and made impotent by the shadows of fear and anxiety, by the shadows of doubt and self-contempt. For the shadow of doubt falls often

> Between the motion
> And the act
>
> Between the emotion
> And the response

Chirico's straw-filled doll is pinioned to an armature in the city square, alone and desolate in the very sight of a majestic and vigorous past. Chirico's painting is a plastic statement of our distance (in emotional perspective) from the wisdom of ancient Greece, from the castles of Provence, from the glory that was the human figure in the Renaissance, from the glory that was the human spirit in Homer and Sophocles.

Design invariably, from the simplest to the most complex, has meaning. Design is metaphorical, just as language is metaphorical. Patterns, shapes, and outlines express inner thoughts and feelings, give body and form to beliefs and doubts, hopes, ideals, needs. Design is informed thought or emotion, an allegory of that which is within us. Design is communication and is surrogate for the something within which, curiously, is not fully created until it has been given expression formally. Hence design is a making of something, the creation of a pattern which represents the thought or feeling, and at the same time becomes a something in itself, a captured, embodied emotion. In this sense all design is representational. For all design is emblematic of the thought of the designer and says something about him and his society. Design is never really random or accidental or pure. It always has meaning. It is always a thought or a feeling becoming substantial. And the substance is the metaphorical expression of the mind's life. The astonishing thing is that the design should so often say so well what we want it to say, so that sometimes the idea or emotion appears to have been perfectly realized in the design.

Before inquiring further into the philosophy of design, let me illustrate the relationship of design to cultural beliefs and social ideals in a specific culture pattern—the genteel tradition in American life.

The genteel tradition in America had its beginnings in the eighteenth century and was the American democratic equivalent of European aristocratic life. The tradition has persevered into our own times (though it has suffered some changes, to be sure), but it was most vigorous in the early nineteenth century. Though the aim of its social philosophy is happiness, and though as a way of life the tradition seeks to avoid the unpleasant, if necessary by overlooking it, nevertheless, the genteel tradition trusts in the good things of life, believes in being civilized, and is devoted, in a naive sort of way, to the idea of good will toward men.

Essential to the tradition is a social homogeneity, defined to a great extent, though not exclusively, by wealth and a community of cultivated tastes. In the late eighteenth century and in the early nineteenth century the ideals of taste were derived from European aristocratic society, and the categories of the cultivated life were expressed with insight by Lord Chesterfield as "les manieres, les agremens, et les graces," as manners, the cultivated pleasures, and the graces.

15

By manners, of course, a great deal more is meant than mere drawing-room poise. By manners is meant that whole social structure implied in the term "good form," form that keeps the world together. Civilization is form, and a civilized society is one that has developed a "style" of behavior, a style made real in ceremony, in social patterns, elegant and complicated, like the figure in the carpet, like a sentence of Henry James.

Form is expressed not only in the ritual of good manners but also in the picturesque, in the composed, or better still, perhaps, in the posed, where space, the space concept, which is basic to the genteel philosophy, is experienced in its deepest sense. Distance lends enchantment to the view, as a genteel poet once said, and the view is of the utmost importance. It is the open window looking out upon the far away in picturesque composition that is the stamp and seal of this philosophy. And out of space is made the ideal, one might almost say, the beauty of the remote, for it is in the remote that the tradition has most to say, believes in most, and serves as its very foundation—whether it be expressed in the view, or the good things which come from far corners of the earth, a Ming porcelain, an Indian tapestry, or whether it is the liberal and charitable interest which one can show for those at some little remove—can show from a distance to the less fortunate of the earth. It is the vista, given out, perhaps, by aisles of honeysuckle or cedar hedges, the vista of misty blue mountains at the end of the aisle or of a classical summer house set in a small court at the end of a pleasant alley, or a vista of the past, of tradition, of history itself, becoming in the hands of the tradition a space idea as much as a time idea, as in scenic wallpaper that pictures clipper ships, and the wide ocean, and, superimposed in the composition, an architectural ruin of ancient Rome.

The feeling is spatial. The ideal is the statuesque, the snap shot, the still life, a kind of frozen space, in which the culture, the vision and image of the good things of life—these parks and parterres and hedges, these views, these ceremonies and rituals of the photograph album, these ancient ruins, abbeys composed in myrtles and ivies, these *objets d'art* from the far corners—are congealed, in which the pleasant, the gracious, the charming, the delightful, the tasteful has been made to abide, to endure, in space forever.

"The failure of Woolett, Massachusetts," says Maria Gostrey in *The Ambassadors*, "was the failure to enjoy," to enjoy, of course, the agreeable things of life, the cultivated pleasures, as Lord Chesterfield called them, for Woolett was puritan minded, and it was against conscience in Woolett to be "happy." In the social philosophy of the genteel tradition, happiness—serene worldly contentment—is of basic importance, and the authentic Brahmin was educated to the tried pleasures, to appreciation of *tradition* (the mellowed past), to taste in the arts, in literature, in the rare and precious.

But when Lord Chesterfield speaks of *les graces,* he touches on the vibrant life of the tradition. The Graces, it will be remembered, are the three goddesses of classical mythology who preside over the elegant and refined pleasures of life, enhancing them with brilliance, joy, and the freshness of bloom. Aglaia is brilliance, attending social enjoyments, present wherever there is good breeding and good nature, lending sprightliness, sparkling wit, and polish to discourse. Euphrosyne stands for joy, one who tones down the Dionysian to acceptable proportions, to tasteful entertainment, who inspires gracious living, a general good will, who gives spice to the agreeable things of life. And Thalia represents innocence and new bloom, the naive, the unsophisticated. She is youth, sweetness, the uncorrupted, the very color and vitality of youth in all its unsmirched blossoming freshness, an adornment, a springtime decoration, a Lady Hamilton as "Nature" by George Romney.

Examples of the genteel tradition in modern painting are to be found in the paintings of Pierre Bonnard, Raoul Dufy, and Henri Matisse. Dufy's *Open Window in Nice* is a polished and felicitous composition. It is a picture of a richly furnished room looking out through open French doors (their long glass windows etched with graceful traceries) upon a Mediterranean scene in profound azure. The room is a tableau, pleasing, sophisticated, reflecting the cultivated sensibilities of those who might really live in such surroundings. But it is the whole painting that delights the eye with subtle harmonies and pleasing

17

patterns suggesting good manners, and, effortlessly, the best of taste. In the paintings of Pierre Bonnard one sees the work of a painter who wished to paint only happy, gracious things, gardens with figures, dinner tables, windows opening out upon quiet landscapes, flowering almond trees. If one analyzes the charm of a Matisse painting, he will find, I think, that it derives from the philosophy of life that emphasizes form—interiors with open windows, decorative figures on ornamental backgrounds (a kind of ceremonial pattern), a cultivated sensibility with experience of the good things (these pineapples and anemones and Japanese objects of art), the pose (the picturesque, the sunlit interior, the still life of flowers and tables and "arrangements," the windows and doors with views, the vista), the remote, that distance that lends enchantment, the exotic—those seraglios and odalisques and arabesques, and Moroccan landscapes, and last but hardly least, the representation of happiness, of the ideal of happiness, that obvious "joy of living" so youthfully expressed, really, in the brilliant colors. The work of art should "not raise problems," said Matisse. "I want people . . . to get a feeling of repose, when looking at my painting." This is the meaning of that exquisite composition, that sorcery of arrangement, that magic of rhythm and color—the genteel philosophy become substance in decorative design.

This, too, is the meaning of magazines like "House and Garden," the statuesque covers of "Harper's Bazaar" and "Vogue," the posed covers, and, as a fine example of the tradition brought well up-to-date, of the late "Flair" magazine of the window-vista covers. This is the meaning of the advertising which occurs in these magazines, of the "pose," the "setting," the photographs of far places, the "snapshot" of the family clustered happily around the expensive automobile drawn up before a Georgian entrance in an expanse of wide green lawns.

This is the meaning of scenic suburbia, of the park-like avenues, the "country" lanes, and the picturesque nautical settings where there is so much of everything to contribute to the happy life, where the environment is, as Matisse said of his paintings, "a cerebral sedative, rather like a comfortable armchair." This is the meaning of interior decor, where elegance is employed as

18

representative of the philosophy of the good things, the discerning, the exotic. This is the meaning of that domestic architecture which we recognize as Georgian, the uttermost in refinement, in harmonious proportions, as in the distinguished work of Samuel McIntire, expressing the whole of a tradition. Georgian architecture is the perfect expression of that "reasonable, delightful order" so dear to the heart, so very much the heart of the genteel tradition.

Our inner thoughts and beliefs become substantial in the works of our hands, and if we wish to know what we deeply believe, what we approve of, we have but to look at the things we have made. Consider, for example, Thoreau's house at Walden Pond, which tells us as much about Concord high thinking as the Craigie house does about Cambridge high living in the nineteenth century. I do not know that Thoreau's house could have been called domestic architecture. It was intended only as a "shelter." But it had meaning nevertheless. The little hut was a representation of the philosophy of New England transcendentalism. Thoreau chose the kind of dwelling which should in no way be a burden to him, as he had some special business to transact with nature and with himself, and he could not spend his time looking after his property. His house was a protest against the materialistic way of life where "things" count for more than people. But it was more than that. It was a shelter designed to let the owner live by the seasons, even by the parts of the day, morning, afternoon, evening. It was a shelter that left the spirit free to follow its whims. But it tells us even more. It tells us about New England thrift, of the acceptance of the challenge to make do with little, so that the worldly shall not be more than the spiritual. The little hut had above all something most emphatic to say about freedom. It was James Russell Lowell who passed the judgment on Thoreau's *Walden* that has clung to it ever since its publication. "Thoreau's experiment actually presupposed," said Lowell, "all that complicated civilization which it theoretically abjured."

But it was not Thoreau's distaste for civilization that sent him to Walden Pond. Thoreau wished to live for a while on the shores of Walden Pond to see what it had to offer, just as Lowell wished often to travel in Europe to see what it had to offer. Far from abjuring civilization, it was precisely civilization that Thoreau wanted and approved of, the highest kind of civilization, which makes it possible for a man to go to Walden Pond if his business calls him thither, precisely because the mortar does exist, because lumber is available, and lamps, and ploughs, and books. Civilization makes possible the choice. *To insist through action upon the right to make a choice*—that was the meaning of the house at Walden. Let others do as they wish—make britannia-ware lamps at Brook Farm, enjoy the society of the great country houses of England, worship in churches, count money at high desks, or frequent bar rooms. Thoreau was a naturalist and a philosopher. So he went to Walden to transact his business. And when Thoreau had had enough of Walden, he left, saying he "had several more lives to live and could not spare any more time for that one." It is no wonder that the house at Walden is no longer standing. It was not important that it should stand after Thoreau left it. It was not a monument. It was a shelter only, from which the spirit could roam at will.

As language is different among the different peoples of the world, so design is diversified according to the various cultures of the world. And the masterpieces of design are outward signs of the subjective life of a people, just as the masterpieces of literature are also confessions of the life within. How diverse and numerous are these masterpieces of design is only too well known today as a result of far-reaching studies in archaeology and cultural anthropology. And without exception, each created article of a culture is a figure of speech, a vehicle made to carry inner thoughts and feelings with more or less power and distinction.

The tree of life has been a symbol from time immemorial, signifying man's undying hope to realize the sources of his existence and to become one with them, in this life and in the life hereafter. In different styles and versions, the flowering tree has appeared over the world, in Coptic textiles of the fourth century, in Persian silks carried to Spain, in Indian tapestries, in Chinese porcelains and embroideries, in illuminated Mexican manuscripts.

The bridge, in its many styles and designs, has stood in all lands and times for coherence, for joining and holding together, from the George Washington Bridge in New York to the covered bridges of New England, from Japanese foot bridges to Maillart's sculptured concrete. How deep a meaning one may attach to the bridge can be seen from the dedicated work of John and Washington Roebling in their Brooklyn Bridge; in the stained-glass, cathedral-like design of Joseph Stella's paintings of Brooklyn Bridge; in Hart Crane's epic *The Bridge,* inspired by the Brooklyn Bridge; in Jo Mielziner's stage setting for Maxwell Anderson's *Winterset;* and in the cluster of emotions attached to Brooklyn Bridge by the people of the Boroughs of Brooklyn and Manhattan.

There is profound religious meaning in the design of a Cambodian temple, just as there is in the design of a medieval cathedral and in the Toltec Avenue of the Dead. There is cultural meaning in the construction of a Malayan house on stakes, and in the cliff-dwellings of the Pueblo Indians. Consider how freighted with meaning is the Hiwassee Dam of the Tennessee Valley Authority. Its concrete is reinforced with a philosophy of life. (This is no waste land!) The dam at Hiwassee is a symbol of creativity and cooperation. And the beauty of its engineering derives, in part at least, from what it stands for—unity of purpose among men toward useful and creative and human ends.

Of all design, architecture probably has the most to say metaphorically because it has so much of *history* in it. Architectural design stands for tradition, continuity of human faith, the victory of man over intransigent forces and materials, the past with its wealth of thought and its wealth of feeling. The Greek temple, the Egyptian tomb, the Gothic cathedral—these are the very texture of history, the thought and hope of perpetuation become realized and substantial. The history of Europe is in her ecclesiastical design: Romanesque, containing reminiscences of the Crusades and of Byzantium and the East; Gothic, with its great vaults and stained glass expressive of medieval religious fervor, its slender piers and flying buttresses metaphors in stone of medieval logic; Renaissance, in its rich worldly beauty emblematic of Renaissance humanism; Baroque, a sign of the vastness and grandeur that was the mind of the seventeenth century.

21

The early history of America is clearly presented in New England church architecture, an architectural design embodying all the puritan virtues. In the simple, harmoniously proportioned, many-windowed, steeple-topped, white wooden buildings built to the Glory of God and the Holy Commonwealth is represented divine orderliness and austerity and candor. There is nothing inexplicable here, no flesh, no appetite, no vanity, nor worldly longings. Here is purity and that clear defiant individualism which believes in the unencumbered exploration of the self toward personal salvation, that single-minded pursuit of perfection, that insistence upon personal identity, and that polar solitude which is, to the puritan, of all things most godlike. This church is a part of our history, and even to those who do not take part in its devotions or believe in its philosophy, its architecture is meaningful as history, is full of the ideals of a great tradition. Architecture is not frozen music, but through its symbolic form, it is frozen history.

What, if one stops to think of them, is one to make of his surroundings, the things he looks at, the materials he uses, the objects, breaking up space, in and around which the routine of his daily life takes place? Our environment is inevitably a projection in design of what we believe about life. If we were to choose the modern design which seems to say most about the twentieth century, which appears to be most widespread and meaningful, we would probably select the one that is based on the cube or rectangle, or, reducing the design to its simplest and most telling element, the horizontal straight line. It is tempting tö look for a meaning in the free forms of contemporary design, in the organic line rather than the straight line, in the biomorphic rather than the geometrical pattern. And indeed there is much that is significant socially and psychologically in contemporary abstract painting (in the work of Jackson Pollock, for example), in ceramics, and particularly in sculpture, where the organic form expresses primordial emotions and strange psychological insights with vivid intensity. In fact, the free sensitive organic line has meaning in it as yet incapable of being articulated in social and psychological language. Nevertheless, the most common shapes in modern design are those based on the straight line, and this is most obvious, of course, in modern architecture.

A great deal has already been written about the early history of cubism as a strong and authoritative art movement originating largely with Dutch and Parisian painters in the early part of the century. The social and philosophical meaning of cubism is of chief interest to us here. In many ways the history of the twentieth century has been expressed in modern cubist design. For example, one must observe that it is closely related to theoretical science in its emphasis on a space-time dimension and on the principle of simultaneity; in its research into space, as with Parisian cubism, and into time, as with Italian futurism. One must also be impressed with the cubist's philosophical questioning of reality itself and with the social protest implied in the breaking up (the deformation) of the "old" reality and its rehabilitation into a new, more harmonious composition, that shall be a little nearer the eye's desire if not the heart's.

Yet cubism has even deeper meaning psychologically. The cube, the rectangle, the square and the line are signs of pronounced inner feelings. One would be rash, perhaps, to say "precisely" what these feelings are, for they are clearly not the same to everyone. Yet we may be reasonably certain of this, that linear design is very nearly always symbolic of the intellectual, not as distinguished from the emotional, but as different from the organic or "natural." The straight line stands for basic simplicity, for directional movement (e.g., in the rectangle), for horizontal drive, for a balance of tensions in the right angle, and for crisis, as in the intersection. Specifically, the long straight line of the rectangle stands for energetic horizontal movement. Modern architecture is linear in design, the rectangle being its basic shape. The dynamic character of this horizontal movement, imaginatively pioneered by Frank Lloyd Wright, is an expression of our new inner orientation to the space-time continuum that, when expressed in terms of everyday happenings, is simply a sensitiveness to new energies and to their expression in terms of *speed* and *change*. A feature of modern design is its minimum of detail and ornament, its simplicity and directness, its compelling immediacy, powerful movement in something like Picasso's *Guernica* mural, sudden drama of black and white in interior decoration, instantaneity of appeal in popular advertising. The machine, modern architecture, cubistic abstract painting, bridges, industrial engineering, and advertising design are all emblematic of the new personality which believes in speed and change. Nikolaus Pevsner has described very well what it is we respond to in modern linear design, when, in writing of the work of Walter Gropius, he sáys,

> Glass walls are now clear and without mystery, the steel frame is hard, and its expression discourages all other-worldly speculation. It is the creative energy of this world in which we live and work and want to master, a world of science and technique, of speed and danger, of hard struggles and no personal security, that is glorified in Gropius' architecture. *(Pioneers of Modern Design)*

The straight line is our tree of life. The source of our life and the nourishment of our being appear to derive from the hidden energies of which the horizontal drive is sign and symbol as well as effect—the articulation of speed in the train on the track, the automobile on the parkway, the airplane in its path, the propulsion of the world's commerce from destination to destination across the earth, inflexible and with fierce determination.

But there lingers in one's mind a doubt that modern design can remain purely abstract and intellectual and compulsive in its movement. The feeling for something a little more "human" and less "driven" is being expressed in recent developments in linear design. What may have started as an articulation of speed and change only and for their own sake has been considerably sweetened by the milk of broader social philosophies.

Though we do not respond to the lotus flower or the spreading tree of life, we find spiritual sustenance in certain patterns of cubes and squares and rectangles that are symbolic ritual performances of *freedom*. The line is authority, *but space is freedom*. The tension between space and boundary is fully suspended in the square, whose right angles are, in effect, movable in any direction, making the possibility of more room everywhere. In modern design, space is not cramped but flexible. Instead of being cabined and confined, we are emancipated emotionally in the feeling of being able, like the cube, to expand limitlessly in all directions simultaneously. The sense of free movement is embodied ideoplastically in the United Nations Buildings in New York. In outer appearance, the Secretariat may resemble a colossal filing cabinet, indifferent to flesh and blood of humans. But when the Secretariat and the Assembly building are seen together (from any position) the design becomes symbolic of free, plastic movement, space expanding with the undulations of the human spirit, flexible and hospitable to human ideas and feelings. It is not without meaning that the United Nations Buildings should be on the bank of a great river, tributary leading to all the corners of the earth, nor in a great city opening out with concourses in every direction. Nor are the spacious foyers, flowing into each other and looking out on so many sides on broad plazas and terraces merely decorative in purpose. The easy gracious movement of ramps and corridors, of outgoing glass walls, of waves of space and open areas bespeak the ideal of the unimpeded flow of people, expanding emotionally to embrace more than ever was embraced before in the history of the world. In this design, symbol of inner hopes and aspirations, we can be reassured that people are striving still for freedom. So too in much contemporary domestic architecture we find this understanding of ideal human wants. In the work of Marcel Breuer, Mies Van der Rohe, Philip C. Johnson, Charles Eames, Richard Neutra, Eric Mendelsohn, Gregory Ain, and many others, we see imaginative expressions of inner ideals of freedom. These architects have been inspired by more than a playing with space, more than with the creation of works of art. As I have said in another place, "Their buildings are materialized philosophy—the old but still the very best philosophy, the philosophy of freedom. Their creations say that we ought to live in and be surrounded by an environment that makes in every way for the free, uninhibited spiritual growth of each human being, by an environment that encourages each personality to grow and mature. The new philosophy of design, with its intermingling of inner and outer spaces, with its invitation to communicate, with its purity of motive and its spiritual values, is a philosophy of good will out-going to all men." Modern design is a metaphor of our longing for freedom and in many ways an attempt to accomplish this longing in reality.

Design is inspired from within. When we look at nature—sand dunes or mountain lakes, woods, the sea, desert or prairie or upland pasture—we see only those details and make only that arrangement of the parts which will form a hieroglyph of our inner life. Oscar Wilde's paradox that nature imitates art (that a London fog is a copy of a Monet painting) is more than a half truth. It is we who make the design in what we see, and the design is a statement of what we believe. One can make a picture out of the boles of several trees arranged in concert for the eye, as Cezanne painted them, or as one might see them in a public park or through one's picture window. Or we can draw a shell or a leaf as we see it, or want to see it, so that our drawing shall be a pictorial representation of our thoughts about the leaf, adding tone and color and *chiaroscuro* to give depth and subtlety to the meaning we are imparting. And when we choose our surroundings (if we have a choice), we choose intentionally and according to our prejudice the cottage by the waterfall or the city apartment, and we decorate these dwelling places with our cherished beliefs as well as with our dearest possessions.

To have no taste, say interior decorators, is inexcusable. It is worse than bad taste. For no taste implies no beliefs about life. Tastes vary, however, for we are not inclined to agree about the details or the ultimate nature of the good life. Just as men speak their ideals with many tongues, so men speak their ideals in many patterns of design. Health and pleasure arise from the infinite variety that is called forth in the articulation of the ideal; and we turn to the myriad expressions of this various world for refreshment, for beauty, and, really, for a better understanding of the ideal thoughts of the mind of man.

Metaphor In Everyday Speech

> *"The commonest metaphors would be questioned [by Mr. Kilpatrick] till some bitter truth had been forced from its hiding place 'Those fiendish German atrocities——' 'But are not fiends a figment of the imagination?' 'Very well, then; these brutal atrocities——' 'But none of the brutes does anything of the kind!' 'Well, what am I to call them?' 'Is it not plain that we must call them simply human?'"*
>
> C. S. LEWIS, *Surprised by Joy*

THE LANGUAGE most of us use to conduct our everyday affairs is a plain and practical language. Yet except for matter-of-fact information, this everyday language is surprisingly metaphorical. The words *up* and *down*, for instance, may signify literally an upward motion toward the sky, as in climbing a ladder or being *upstairs*, or may signify a downward motion toward the earth, as in falling from a ladder or coming downstairs, or a downward motion into the earth, as in digging a hole. On the other hand, the words *up* and *down* are often used figuratively, and it appears that in our human condition, it is as a rule very much better to be *up* than *down*.

Consider, for instance, the importance to the employee of *moving up* to a *higher* position; observe the misfortune of *coming down* in the world, of *falling down* in the estimation of others, of being *down-and-out* (where the *out* adds something more to being merely down), that diplomatic talks *break down*, that human beings have nervous *breakdowns*; observe that we do not like to be *looked down on*, or to be at the *bottom* of the heap, or to be *low* in our mind, or to get *low* grades in school, or to have it said of us that we are *low born* or *low bred*. According to Milton's *Paradise Lost* certain angels *fell* and were a long time falling from a lofty height to the bottomless pit. Metaphorically (and perhaps literally!) the greatest adversity ever visited upon man was his *fall* from grace.

If we may judge from everyday speech, it is better to be *up;* in a sense to be on top of the world, or at least on top of the heap, is best and most desired. We do not like to be *cracked down on;* we prefer to get a *lift* from something, and on occasions we seek to be *uplifted.* In the hierarchy of the industrial and political worlds, it is better to be *above* or *over* someone than to be *under* or *below* someone; in the everyday world of business, to *take over* is certainly preferable to *going under.* To be *top* man, or at least to be one of the *higher-ups* is best. *High living,* whatever else one may say of it (that like pride it goeth before a fall), appears to be enviable, along with *high-powered* automobiles and *high-priced* clothes. In the eighteenth century *high* living took place *above* stairs, while the servants *below* stairs enacted the roles of the *lower life,* performing their own high jinks. Observe also how it is better to be *above* certain kinds of behavior, above envy, for instance, and also how it is desirable to be *above* the crowd, *au-dessus de la melee.* For Goethe, it is *above* the tree tops and mountain tops where one feels there is that long-sought peace which is eventually to be the possession of everyman.

The reader will remember for himself countless examples of linguistic highs and lows, ups and downs, aboves and belows that have come to his attention. But there are other illustrations of this common metaphorical usage which ought not to be neglected here. There is the *ladder* to *success* and there is the social *climber.* *High-minded* is an epithet of approbation, while *low-minded* is a term of opprobrium. In *Supreme* Court, the adjective derives from the Latin *supremus,* meaning *above, higher,* as do also the words *superior* and *superiority.* There are *emotional heights* and *intellectual heights,* and there is the well-known admonition that in certain circumstances one should exercise *mind over matter.* In our language we use *high* and *highest* to signify the very best, the most worthy and estimable, that to which we must pay our respect if not unquestioning obedience. *Your Eminence* is the title of honor given to a cardinal of the Roman Catholic Church; *Your Royal Highness* is the form of address accorded a royal personage. And *ascent* is preferable to *descent,* as a rule, though *ascend* has a connotation and a richness of meaning which goes beyond mere up and down, so ennobled is the word by religious associations.

There are exceptions to the goodness of *up* and to the baseness (French *bas,* meaning low) of *down.* If one flies too high, like Icarus he may get his wings scorched and fall to destruction. And it is dangerous to be too keyed up—one might snap, like the string of a musical instrument. Moreover, to *settle down,* especially at a certain age, is generally considered advisable; to be *down to earth* signifies stability, solidity; and *going to the root* of the matter is a proper strategy. The epithet *deep* is often applied as a term of approval, as in *deep thinker;* and *getting to the bottom of things*—to the hidden—is commonly advised as a sound approach to recondite or confused transactions.

But why should it be better, generally speaking, to be *up* than *down,* to be *high* rather than *low?* Why has the everyday speech of a people chosen *high* or *up* to signify that which is good and *low* or *down* to signify that which is as a rule to be avoided? (Our thinking and our speech, it would seem, are still very much bound by the Cartesian coordinates of height and depth, length and breadth.) The metaphorical usage of these words is drawn, or would certainly appear to be drawn, from human experience. In everyday experience it is better, or so it would seem, to be *over* other people rather than *under* them— literally, of course, to be in a position of power in terms, finally, of brute strength. If we might for a moment think of the social order as a pyramid with a sharp peak, the best position would be, apparently, at the top where there is room for only one person. This position is marked by loneliness and solitude, but it is nevertheless, or seems nevertheless to be, an enviable position, since so many people strive for it. *It is a position of power; but power is only a means of achieving a high degree of solitude.*

The desire to be alone, or nearly alone, is not so uncommon nowadays as one might suppose. The base of the social pyramid is characterized by rampant competition, and the constant threat to personal uniqueness. In our everyday speech we give ourselves away, as it were. The desire to preserve unaffected our individuality and our identity is more than a cultural ideal; it appears to be an existential fact. And in order to preserve our individuality, we must be powerful enough to rise *above* others. (Of course, no one ever achieves that position where he is highest of all. The movement upward toward the empyrean is a matter of degree, and if the mountain top is too rare or chilly an atmosphere, the penthouse or the house-on-the-hill will satisfy.)

It seems simply to be true that there are more people in the low places, fewer people in the high places and that it is better both socially and geographically to be where there are fewer people. *High*, used metaphorically, is only a way of saying there are fewer people around. And as we still look upon life as a struggle for existence, to be high up is to be above, literally, the struggle.[1]

If one stops to examine everyday speech critically, he may be astonished to find out how loose it is, inexact, disconnected, fuzzy. Mostly we conduct our affairs on the fringe of thought. It is only when we isolate experience intellectually that we engage in linguistic refinements. Indeed, there is seldom call to delineate sharply, and we appear often actually to flourish in the verbal mist. Only in the domain of the exact sciences are we very fine in our measurements; only in the fields of humane learning and the arts are we subtly discriminating. Moreover, outside the domain of science and the arts we are mostly a little mistaken, are only approximate and partial, about everything, excepting, of course, in the references we make to the basic requirements of survival, such as choosing between edible and poisonous foods. In everyday life when we are not making an effort to be lucid and to put our thoughts into scrupulously logical order, they seem indeed to be vague, mere guesses or sighs or phatic sounds that vanish like puffs of smoke in the air. Yet we

---

[1]"They all strive to be rich. Why? Did you ever ask yourself? For power, of course. But especially because wealth shields from immediate judgment, takes you out of the subway crowd to enclose you in a chromium-plated automobile, isolates you in huge protected lawns, Pullmans, first-class cabins. Wealth, *cher ami,* is not quite acquittal, but reprieve, and that's always worth taking." From *The Fall* by Albert Camus, trans. by Justin O'Brien (New York, 1957), p. 82.

manage, roughly, to get along. Indeed, this gossamer obscurity at the border between thought and vacuity, this vagueness at the margin, may be a kind of protection against mental rigidity, against making up our minds too soon, indulging in over-simplified evaluations. It is as necessary for thought as for anything else in human experience that it shall grow and mature.

In any event, it is perhaps on the linguistic edges, on the intellectual fringe, where we find the kind of language that tells us most about ourselves as a people. As we have seen, *high* and *low* are vague terms (we do not know exactly how high we mean nor how low), but they are enough to indicate direction. They reveal hidden wishes and ideals that are quite readily understood by others in communication.

Study for a moment the word *beyond*. Like *high* and *low* the word is a space metaphor which appears to signify a remove in distance so far as to be outside the area of our known world. It may not always be desirable to be beyond; but that there is a beyond, a mysterious *other*, we do not, apparently, doubt. For there are things *beyond belief*, there is the life *beyond life*, there are ideas *beyond our understanding;* at times our condition is *beyond hope, beyond cure*, our state *beyond endurance*. Nietzsche looked beyond good and evil, Freud carried his speculations beyond the pleasure principle, and O'Neill created characters who dreamed of places beyond the horizon. The lure of far places is very potent, though fear of the unknown may often stay our steps at the threshold of the yonder.

Closely related to *beyond* as a metaphor is the concept of motion forward, as in *moving forward* with one's work, *moving on* to another idea or thought (or to the next world), of *getting on* in the world, or *getting ahead*. Sometimes a statement of progress is intended as saying we are nearing the completion of an assigned task, where the boundaries are more or less clearly drawn. But in many instances the metaphor is used loosely to imply motion forward to a destination which is but dimly seen and dimly apprehended, though because the movement is said to be *forward*, it is therefore good and acceptable. Like many other "fillers" common to everyday speech, these phrases like *getting ahead* have become mere gestures (like the gestures for *go away* or *come here*) and are not, perhaps, language at all in the systematic sense.

Consider also the figurative aspect of a phrase like *advancement of education.* Though we have come to use phrases like this rather widely, we do not, I suspect, mean by them *motion forward;* in instances like this we equate advancement with increase, and perhaps that is what we ought to say. We want more education, both in quantity and quality. We haven't really the slightest idea where education is *going.* Latterly, the concept of *development* has become a common substitute for *advancement,* and the difference in meaning is notable. For development (with its evolutionary connotations) suggests *growth* or *change* into new and more complicated forms, implying the notion of improvisation (experiment) as the method of change. At any rate, the concept of development suggests change rather than goal. And change, to us, is more devoutly to be wished than for something to end. Not to know where we are going in any branch of human endeavor may well be in the nature of things. Perhaps all we mean by moving forward is that we can't do otherwise, time always seeming to imply a destination, fixed and predestined. And just as *forward* is always good (except when used to describe a pert and saucy child), so *backward* is always bad. To go backward (or to retreat) is to move from a better to a worse state, as the dictionary says.

But for the most part, metaphors of motion forward signify to us a desire for change of place or condition. We are committed to change and believe deeply in the efficacy and value of change. As a rule we do not like where we *are,* or someone else does not like where we are. Hence to change position is sufficient reason for *moving on.* "Keep moving," says the policeman and the entrepreneur. We do not advise, as Yeats does in "A Prayer for My Daughter," being rooted in "one dear perpetual place," nor as does Simone Weil in *The Need for Roots*—"To be rooted is perhaps the most important and least recognized need of the human soul." Instead, it is our predilection to advise *more* and *further*—and *further* is *beyond*—but where? "Out of reach"? Few indeed will question the rightness of technological change; but who can outline the end toward which this change is lead-

32

ing? It may well be, of course, that we are not goal-minded at all, that we are indifferent about the destination, that change in itself is quite enough and is all that matters. It is at least a potent weapon against boredom. Perhaps, influenced as we are by language itself, we are the victims of an erroneous notion (that change is always good everywhere) because it has been perpetuated by thoughtless repetition in idiomatic daily speech.

Incidentally, it is revealing to note that poets seldom (at least so far as a cursory inquiry discloses) use such words as *high, low, up, down, small, strong, weak,* etc., in the metaphorical senses we have been discussing. They mostly use these words only in their literal sense, as though that were the only proper way to use them; as metaphors they are either too vague or empty or uncommunicative on the poetic level. Indeed, the poet's strength comes from his very careful and exact use of the literal and concrete meanings of words, surprising as this may at first thought appear. It is literature that keeps language correct as well as expressive, not the patois of our daily talk.

Nevertheless, the patois has its place, for through it we can discern our ideals and our habitual, unexamined beliefs. Consider the words *big, great, small, strong, weak, soft, hard.* A *big* man in industry or in government or in a labor union is called big because he has power of position once accorded perhaps only the stout and muscular. Big men, literally speaking, are stronger, more powerful, than small men. A big man is more dangerous with his fists. He may become the boss by virtue of his large size. We have carried the idea of literal bigness (in size and bulk) over to forms of leadership and responsibility. The metaphor is apparent and it is based on the admiration we cherish for brawn. Our approval of brute strength may be measured by extent of violent gross power displayed and enjoyed daily in comic books, in television, in motion pictures. A *big* man in some enterprise may be a small man literally, but he can exact the same servility from his underlings as the bully who smashes recalcitrant followers in the face.

Bigness is always and everywhere good (except perhaps in women's wrist watches) because it stands for power. And our use of language reflects this approval. There is *big* business, a *big* deal, a mental *giant*, the *big* wheel, a man of *substance*, where substance implies *weight*. (Compare the use of *light weight*, and in general the plus value of *heaviness*.) If the big is good, the small is usually bad, as, morally speaking in the *small* man, or in *small* minded, though for the most part we use other words, like *little* or *nothing* or *nobody* to indicate our contempt for the ineffectual and powerless. Our everyday use of words tells us about ourselves. In general we admire the large size because it means power and power means superiority, means being *above*, or *out of reach*, of the crowd.

The word *great* is so common in everyday speech as to have lost most of its expressiveness and most of the subtle shades of meaning it once contained. For the most part great signifies that which is of more than ordinary size. That which is called *great* is good because it is large, like a great stomach or the Great Wall of China, or the Great Bear, or, in terms of power, the Great Mogul, or in terms of value a *great* work of art, a *great* fortune. A writer's *greatest* work (his *magnum opus*) is usually his most sizeable. We still cling to other meanings of the word, as in *great guy*, where the adjective signifies generosity, likeableness, ability, even humility (though the sense here is often sentimental), as in the *great* man, where the adjective expresses something of the notion of nobility, loftiness of character, or even eminence in point of achievements. But for the most part, *great* carries the connotation of bigness simply in the scale of measurement as opposed to smallness. (If one may say so, the word *great* ought to be used sparingly and correctly in honor of its long history. It has been used with real effectiveness when it refers specifically to a person great with emotion, or courage, or anger, or pride, or arrogance; its history includes the meaning "coarse of grain or texture," big in diet, thick and massive, and pregnant, as in "great with child," which meaning descends to us, along with great emotion or great action, from the Middle English. When Lemuel Gulliver in Swift's *Gulliver's Travels* describes the complexion of the diminutive people of Lilliput he says it appeared to him "the fairest in the world; and talking upon this subject with a person of learning there, who was an intimate friend of mine, he said that my face appeared much fairer and smoother when he looked on me from the ground, than it did upon a nearer view when I took him up in my hand and brought him close, which he confessed was at first a very shocking sight. He said he could discover great holes in my skin; that the stumps of my beard were ten times stronger than the bristles of a boar, and my complexion made up of several colours altogether disagreeable: although I must beg leave to say for myself, that I am as fair as most of my sex and country." When Swift says *great* holes, he uses the word with telling exactness in the obsolete sense of "coarse grained.")

Our metaphors are often drawn from the empirical observations we make of the physical world around us. For instance, normally we prefer that which is *hard* to that which is *soft,* or at least so our figurative language would imply. *Soft* suggests the yielding, the pliant, and the flabby as the opposite of *hard* which suggests the firm and inflexible, the stony and intractable. Of course, a *soft* job is more to be desired than a *hard* job, *soft* voices are more appealing to the ear, the *softness* of the feminine body is alluring, and *soft* music is often agreeable (though we probably ought to say *quiet* instead of *soft* when we are speaking of degrees of sound). Nevertheless, the *soft* is generally thought of as applying to the irresolute, the easily manipulated, submissive, harmless (as in *soft drink*) and, at its extreme, the rotten and squashy, as in overripe fruit. The *hard* is generally admired, as signifying indestructibility, in, for instance, and markedly, *hard cash,* or in the *hard* man who drives a *hard* bargain, or particularly in the derivative *hardy,* meaning that which is not easily destroyed by the opposition, whatever the opposition may be. It may often mean protection, as in the *hard task master* who must be hard in order to train (and ultimately defend) those in his care or charge. The boss *has* to be *hard* we say. *Tough* is closely allied to *hard* and *weak* to *soft.* As a rule, *tough* (except when referring to steak or to the tough guy who is a hoodlum or thug) is an epithet of approval, while *weak* is almost invariably an adjective of contempt or reproach, whether it applies to the supports of a bridge or to a defect in human character. It describes that which is untrustworthy in our everyday affairs. To be *tough* is to be unyielding, whether it be spoken of a tree that withstands the shocks and buffeting of meteorological weather, or of a person who withstands (that is, stands upright against) the shocks and buffeting of the social weather. To be *tough* is to be *hard,* to have the strength to carry a heavy strain and not to break, crack, split or splinter. *Toughness* and *hardness* when applied to human character are tactile metaphors carried over from materials which resist fracture. In general we consider it virtuous to be unyielding, unbending, not to *give in.* Though we are aware in an unconscious sort of way that the rigid or *hard* in the puritanical sense, the aggressive and hard in the frontier sense, are not so successful in the long run as the flexible and easy, nevertheless, hardness and toughness are often approved of to the point where insensitivity, bigotry, crudeness, even brutality are considered of positive worth and of manly quality.

The words *in* and *out* have a wide-ranging metaphorical content, and from them, when they are used figuratively, we learn that as a rule it is better to be *in* than to be *out.* To be *on the inside* is good, for one learns many things there that it profits one to know. *Insiders* usually have valuable information to which *outsiders* enjoy no access. Information is the chief weapon of the *insiders,* and a very powerful weapon it is indeed. Sociologists have expanded at length upon the social value of being one of the *in* group; the experience of each of us has been quite sufficient to teach the bitter meaning of the word *outsider.*

The figurative uses of *in* and *out* are probably drawn from the social relationships of human beings, though they may derive also from the position of the human being in distress of weather. During a storm or under the heat of the sun or in suffering the cold blasts of winter, one is better off *inside* than *outside,* under cover of some safe shelter, though it be only a cave or a hut. Of course, there are instances where it is better to be outside than inside. It is, for example, a happier circumstance to be outside jail than inside. (Note that one is not *kicked out* of jail; one is *sprung*—released, like a bird from a cage.) The modern phrase to be *out of this world* signifies an ideal and a much to be desired position; but in this phrase the world is thought of as a prison, and to be out of it is better than to be in it, for to be out of it is to be *wholly free* of its pain and suffering.

It is good, of course, to be *out of danger,* as it is also good to be *out of trouble,* removed, that is, from the center of activities inimical to man. But for the most part to be *in* is more devoutly to be wished than to be *out.*[2] To be *in the know,* to be *in favor,* to dwell with the *inner* life as richly abundant of meaning and truth, to have access to the *inner sanctum,* to be *in* a state of grace—all these positions are sought after, and it is hoped will be maintained. *Out,* I think we may say, represents fundamentally a state of *death* or nearness to death. If one is *knocked out,* he is rendered unconscious, that is, made into a state akin to death; if one is *tired out,* he is close to exhaustion or unconsciousness, and the same is true of being *worn out,* or being, in a popular phrase, *out like a light,* which is a vivid folk metaphor descriptive of a state of death. To be *put out* as in baseball is to be sent from the field, away from the center of meaningful human activity, to be removed, literally, from the game, that is, from the *game of life.* To be *ousted* from a position or an organization, or to be *kicked out,* even if only from a saloon, is to be placed in an undignified position where shame and insecurity follow consequentially.[3]

Inside is usually the place of safety, the right place to be, sanctuary from evil. In fact, the metaphor of *in-ness* may in the last analysis be a uterine analogy, reference to the birthplace of life. To be *out,* one might almost conclude, is to be dead; to be *in* is to be alive.

It is scarcely necessary to multiply instances of metaphorical usage of the most common words. A compendium of figurative language would include very nearly all words. One or two further illustrations, however, will be sufficient to show that in

---

[2] " . . . the two major parties differ very little in the fundamental principles they profess or the policies they advocate. The chief difference between them is that one is in, or mainly in, and wishes to keep in, while the other is out, or mainly out, and wishes to get entirely in." Carl L. Becker, *Freedom and Responsibility in the American Way of Life* (New York, 1955), p. 94.

[3] Compare such socially meaningful words as *unfrocked, dethroned, deposed, excommunicated.* Modern everyday speech is singularly thrifty of the language and usually prefers the simple *ousted* to locutions of a more learned sort.

our everyday speech the meaning is often in the metaphor though we may not be linguistically conscious of this.

The variations played upon the words *hot* and *cold* tell us a good deal about ourselves. We disapprove of the *hot-headed* and the *cold-hearted*. We approve of the *cool-headed* and the *warm-hearted*. The *cold reception* is unpleasant; the *warm greeting* is pleasant. Popular metaphors of everyday speech very often reflect our use of the humanistic measurement in evaluating human experience. As human beings we instinctively avoid the extremes of heat and cold; in these sensations we prefer moderation—we do not like to be in *hot water* nor to have *cold water* thrown on our plans; we avoid the *heated discussion* and we know what it means to be *frozen with fear*. We like to keep our friendships *warm*, and we like to remain *cool and composed* in an emergency. Where language is humanistically orientated, we may expect to find it at its most rational.

The word *square* signifies almost without exception that which is acceptable.[4] The phrases *on the square, square meal, square deal, square away, square shooting, four square,* and *to square accounts,* or *to square up with* are commonly employed metaphors of approval. The literal geometrical square is almost universally admired for its exactness, its simplicity, its orderliness. It is pragmatically clear and useful, and it has about it a logic that is congenial to the human mind. The square is neat and tidy; it is completely under control.

The modern world (since the time of the Middle Ages) has urged the use of language to settle social differences, as being more civilized than the use of muscle. As a result, linguistically, we have *big talk, brave words, weak argument, small talk, strong words;* we know that words can *hurt, wound our feelings,* if not our persons. Before going in to his mother to scold her for what he considers her bad behavior, Hamlet says, "I will speak daggers to her, but use none." One remembers the old saying: "Sticks and stones will break my bones, but words can never hurt me." It is not true, of course. Words can be *biting*, remarks can

---

[4]Except for the language of the hipster, where *square* is an epithet of contempt, applied usually, I believe, to the insensitive, stuffy, convention-abiding man.

be *cutting*, a speech can be *withering*, *damaging*, a tone of voice can be *murderous*. We speak sometimes with *sharp tongues*, or our talk may be *poisonous* or our *pens drip vitriol* or we destroy with a *torrent of words*. It is perfectly possible to be beaten into insensibility (or imbecility) by words, as witness the young wife in John Osborne's *Look Back in Anger*. Generally speaking, we have substituted words for blows, a very acceptable substitution on the whole. It is natural, therefore, that our metaphors of hurtful talk should be drawn very nearly without exception from the infliction of physical wounds, and this suggests that though we do not literally wound our enemies, we still desire to hurt them. But fortunately our latest weapon, words, is less sanguinary than swords and guns.[5]

Despite the complicated industrial, technological, political, and social environment with which we have surrounded ourselves—in spite of the abundance of our learning, the universality of education, and the ever-increasing bulk of literature about everything—it would appear from casual observation that everyday figurative language is drawn largely from the most commonplace of everyday human relationships and natural happenings. Average daily human talk is distinguished not by its complexity but by its simplicity.[6] Everyday human discourse is not only

---

[5]"Language may be compared with the spear of Amfortas in the legend of the Holy Grail. The wounds which language inflicts upon the thought of man can be healed only by language itself." "Language as Communication" by Ruth Nanda Anshen, in *Language: An Enquiry Into Its Meaning and Function*, ed. Ruth Nanda Anshen (New York, 1957).

[6]Our age especially is not notable for flourishes of rhetoric in everyday spoken language. We usually follow an economy of scarcity in our everyday speech, as though there were but a few hundred words in the language instead of nearly a million. We deliberately choose to speak in staccato monosyllables, giving such color to them as a tone of voice or added gesture will supply. We wish, apparently, to be functional in speech as well as in everything else; our linguistic thrift is a technique of efficiency, a way of getting things done fast. We have reduced the language to a few tokens which we use like well-worn ballots in the day's conversations to show very simply and quickly our approval or disapproval of whatever candidate is at the moment up for inspection. For instance, a thing is either good or bad (if it is not good, it must be bad); either we *see the light* or we are *in the dark;* behavior is either right or wrong; things are either real or imaginary; a person is either educated (meaning he has been to college) or he is uneducated; a person is either bright or stupid, gentle

unadorned, it is fundamentally uncertain and unsophisticated. Perhaps this is purposeful among human beings; at least the situation appears not to have changed, to date, in the recorded history of mankind. It may well be that individual human relationships, unlike vast social organizations, do not call for niceties of expression which would only hinder and get in the way of everyday communication. Art is long, but today is slipping perceptibly and rapidly away. The great works of learning prepare us in quiet for the choice we must make in action, for the choice which must be made without benefit of further discussion. We cannot carry on our daily business of survival in the language of the essay or the novel, nor do we wish to. Words in everyday speech are like acts themselves and stand for acts or for signals and warnings of future acts. The language of everyday speech is the language of action and not of reflection. It is understandable therefore that the metaphors we use should be drawn from human acts and attributes, from the most common of events and experiences—water, cold, heat, earth, sky, food, shelter, clothing, trees, plants, movement, stillness, struggle, love, people, birth, the human body, death, storms, trees, plants, up, down, over, under, in, out. There are for example, *dead issues,* the *dead pan,* the *deadline,* the being *dead right,* the *kiss of death,* the *deathly stillness,* the *deadly enemy;* the *birth* of an idea, the *death* of an institution; there is the fight without fists; there is the hurt without the infliction of a wound; to *by-pass* means to pass by; sometimes we are *out of line,* or a part of the *main line,* or we follow the *party line,* or come to the *end of the line,* or present a *new line* of goods; some alliances make our hands *clean,* some make our hands *dirty;* sometimes we pray that *our hearts may be made clean* within us; we speak of moral values as being *black* or *white;* we speak of differences in terms of *night* and *day;* there is the *fallen idol* with *feet of clay,* the *fall guy,* the *fall from grace,*

---

or rough, phony or O.K., work is work and play is play. We do not wish to distinguish very nicely or at length in choosing alternatives. We are not interested in improvising, in developing our themes, in expanding our hypotheses, in elaborating a thought with chiaroscuros of meaning. We prefer, perhaps, to put things in their places and to leave them there. The metaphorical content of the simplest words becomes frozen into conventional plus and minus values.

the *fallen enemy;* we like to be *backed up* by someone or something; we *rise* to the occasion, we *nourish* our minds; we make a *slip* which is not always on the proverbial banana peel; our feelings are *hurt;* we behave like *curs* or *wasps* and are *currish* or *waspish;* we take a *stand,* or we *backslide;* we are *trapped,* our minds are *poisoned,* we are *sick at heart.* And what would we do without *point of view,* that celebrated promontory from which the individual surveys the world of thought? What would we do without *point* in any of its many uses—*my point is, that's the point, to make a point, to come to the point.*

It is not my intent to compile a dictionary of metaphor, though it is probably clear by now that we could examine thousands of words for their figurative as well as for their literal content. *Slave, fog, crazy, bottleneck, dope, nest, leak, factory hand, sharp pain, heavy heart, open mind, brood, bankrupt, fruitful, role, clockwork, prison, crushed, belt line, louse, darkness, mask, home, in a rut*—these words are surrogates for realities which we experience daily. We could ask of each word how it has come to mean what it means for its users (ask, that is, about its metaphorical history in relation to social beliefs and ideals), and, what is more important, we could ask what the word tells us (*because* it is used metaphorically) about those who use it. Words like *trap, puzzle, snag, unravel, knotty* remark in their various contexts upon the anatomy of frustration, different in kind and degree, perhaps, for different times and places. Words like *drama* and *game* with their reference to life experiences are rich and varied in meaning and, when used metaphorically, are profoundly revealing of our social structure, our behavior, the rules and regulations by which we carry on our daily tasks and perform our daily rituals.[7]

Words like *flame* and *fire* are revealing in the metaphorical sense. The *flame of life* may glow, strive, shoot upward; the flame may be extinguished, as a candle is snuffed *out.* Indeed, so common is the comparison between fire and life (especially among poets) that a linguist might more than half suspect the

---

[7]The often-repeated contemporary metaphor of the *game* with its rules, goals, and strategies, and the related tacit assumptions of role-playing, is a modern sociological insight into ourselves and our behavior.

fire of the extensional world to be the *same as* (though in a different phase) the inner fire of life that has been observed intuitively by the poet, which can consume as well as nourish. Words like *path* and *way* and *branch*, when they are used metaphorically (one might almost s:.y mimetically) with reference to the life of man, betray a quite remarkable parallel to the events of external nature. Metaphors drawn from weather and the seasons, such as *stormy* and *wintry* when applied to the human personality, or words like the *autumn of life* and the *springtime of life* when applied to the human passage through time, are, as we know, plentiful, and they reveal our awareness of nature and our closeness to nature.

If time permitted, we could inquire into those metaphors drawn from the many specialized departments of human thought, from theology, the physical and biological sciences, from medicine,[8] philosophy,[9] law, engineering, the world of business and industry. Modern psychology has supplied us with metaphors in abundance. Psychological categories—the concepts that deal with mental and emotional phenomena—appear to be more meaningful, or more interesting, to us today than the categories of nature—concepts dealing with natural happenings—which were more meaningful or interesting in the centuries before the twentieth. Words from the vocabulary of Freudian psychoanalysis

---

[8]In an essay by John Wain entitled "Along the Tightrope" (in *Declaration,* ed. Tom Maschler [New York, 1958]), there occurs an amusing passage dealing with lay and journalistic views of modern medicine of which the following is an excerpt: "Nature, too weak and faulty to defend herself, is open to the assaults of hostile bacteria, which can only be combated by training a specially ferocious brand of antibiotics, like ferrets, to hunt them down. So the new wonder-drugs succeed each other at intervals of a few months; a new one is tried, it gobbles up the bacteria, the symptoms vanish, a victory is proclaimed in military metaphor ('such-and-such a disease is *conquered*'), and Nature is properly in her place. But of course, before the ink is dry on the newspapers that celebrate this victory, the evil bacteria have gone home and put on a new uniform to reappear as something else— a new set of symptoms to be isolated and attacked. On with the job!—train a new cageful of ferrets! There's no nonsense here about Nature and her benevolence. If a man is ill, the answer is to pump him full of some chemical concoction whose job it is to get in there and work."

[9]Consider, for instance, the language of Existentialism. The metaphorical content of words like *nausea, dread, uneasiness, crisis, estrangement, the absurd* is full of meaning for our times.

are distinctly metaphorical. A glossary of these terms would present us with a running commentary on what we think of ourselves. Words like *conflict, repression, infantilism, split personality, unconscious, censor* are subject to considerable analysis themselves in terms of our lives in society today.

There is one last example which I find irresistible. The verb *brainwash* is a newly-minted metaphor that suggests a clearing of the mind of all previously held beliefs. But is it possible to wash away beliefs, in the same way, for example, as it is possible to wash old newspapers of their ink and then to print new words on the fresh newsprint, as though the old had never existed? *Brainwash* is related to the philosophical metaphor of the *tabula rasa*. If, at birth, the mind is a clean tablet upon which is to be written the experience gained through the senses, then it would seem reasonable to suppose that the slate, or *blackboard,* could be washed clean at any time. But suppose the mind is *not* like a fresh tablet at birth, suppose we think of it as *like* something else. There are many possible analogies (very significantly, in our time, the Freudian concept of the "libido" as a *reservoir* of psychic energy and the Jungian concept of a collective unconscious). There is, also, for example, the Platonic epistemology. If we believe in the philosophy of Socrates and Plato, we shall have to assume that brainwashing is impossible, for the deepest, most divine ideas are a part of us always.

But if we accept behavioristic philosophies, we may say that for all practical purposes at least, we can be mechanically indoctrinated, our minds written upon and erased over and over again. We may not know for a fact what the mind is like, but our behavior will be reflected in what we *think* it is *like.* It is not, perhaps, the validity of the metaphor that is in question, it is rather a matter of what we *do* when we believe in the metaphor. And where it is desired that the beliefs and attitudes of a person shall be subject to manipulation and transformation, the figure of the washable brain will probably serve most usefully.

In conclusion, I should like only to repeat what by now is obvious, that figurative language is the home of many a deep-seated, unexamined belief or mental attitude. In our daily speech are reflected the outlines, at least, of our thoughts and attitudes.

Both speech and thought are often fuzzy and vague, often poverty-stricken, often mere counters of approval or disapproval, often abstractions that have lost their power of expressiveness. But if there is meaning at all, it is in the metaphor still.

Symbols in Literature and Art

T HE MOST commonly used means of communication is, of course, language. We use language every day, assuming that because of it we can converse with others with little danger of being misunderstood. The dictionary is accessible to all, and it would seem that words mean what they mean. But very often our use of words is ambiguous, vague, and irresponsible; this is sometimes because of ignorance or illiteracy, but just as often it is a deliberate intention. When Alice professes not to understand Humpty Dumpty's use of words, he presents the case for caprice with considerable logic:

> 'There are three hundred and sixty-four days when you might get un-birthday presents—'
> 'Certainly,' said Alice.
> 'And only *one* for birthday presents, you know. There's glory for you!'
> 'I don't know what you mean by "glory" ' Alice said.
> Humpty Dumpty smiled contemptuously. 'Of course you don't—till I tell you. I meant "there's a nice knockdown argument for you!" '
> 'But "glory" doesn't mean "a nice knock-down argument," ' Alice objected.
> 'When *I* use a word,' Humpty Dumpty said in rather a scornful tone, 'it means just what I choose it to mean—neither more nor less.'
> 'The question is,' said Alice, 'whether you *can* make words mean so many different things.'
> 'The question is,' said Humpty Dumpty, 'which is to be master—that's all.'

Very often *we* are the master. Yet it is the virtue and strength of language even at its most impressionistic and evocative that it is intended to serve in close correspondence to the realities of human experience. Language is surely our most useful way of communicating ideas, but like democracy, we must be eternally vigilant in our protection of it.

However, a meaning is not always conveyed by words, and talking with one another is not always done with words. Though we suppose that the meaning of signs and symbols is not so definitely fixed as the meaning for words, a little inquiry into the nature of signs and symbols will show us, I think, that they have an intrinsic meaning that words cannot have. Consider, for instance, the meaning conveyed by traffic lights. These signs are acutely exact, and they communicate meaning virtually without ambiguity. They are not rich in meaning, but their meaning is unmistakable. Recall with what astonishment Robinson Crusoe recognized the human footprint in the sand. Under the circumstances, the footprint was a fixed sign incapable of being misread, and it was the exactness of the sign which was responsible for the depth of Robinson Crusoe's emotional reaction. Since they often embody their meaning within their shape and form, signs and symbols are more precise in meaning than words. That is, they are already, in part at least, what they stand for. In the very act of symbolizing or signifying, they *are* what they represent. The symbol is the thing it stands for, and when the symbol is at once a symbol and the thing it stands for, it is itself a reality, and its meaning is conveyed with the force of an event. An example will serve to clarify this idea.

Toward the end of Sir Thomas Malory's *Le Morte D'Arthur* we learn how upon a Trinity Sunday at night King Arthur dreamed that Sir Gawaine came to him and warned him not to fight against Sir Mordred the next day at Salisbury, for as sure as he did, both would be slain, and the most part of their knights. Sir Gawaine advises King Arthur to take a treaty, thus putting in a delay. Waking from his dream, King Arthur sends Sir Lucan and Sir Bedivere to take a treaty with Sir Mordred. Sir Mordred agrees to the armistice and also to hold conference that day with King Arthur in the middle of the field between the two armies. Before King Arthur goes into the field, he warns all his armies that if any should see a sword drawn on the other side, they should "come on fiercely, and slay that traitor, Sir Mordred," for King Arthur did not trust him. Likewise, Sir Mordred warned his host that "should any see a sword drawn, they should come on fiercely and slay all that stood before them, for in no wise did he trust the treaty." No sooner had King Arthur and Sir Mordred met and drawn up an agreement, than an adder came out of a little heath bush and stung a knight (one of the small company in the center of the field) on the foot. The thoughtless knight drew his sword to kill the adder. On both sides the armies saw the sword drawn and forthwith blew their horns and their trumpets. "And so both hosts dressed them together. . . . And never was there seen a more dolefuller battle in no Christian land."

At the end of that unhappy day it came to pass that King Arthur slew Sir Mordred, but in so doing received his own death wound and fell in a swoon to the earth. When he awoke, King Arthur charged the last living of his knights, Sir Bedivere, to take the King's sword Excalibur to the nearby waterside, to throw the sword into the water, then to return to tell him what he saw. Sir Bedivere twice disobeyed his King, so bejewelled was the sword, so beautiful and rare, he could not bring himself to cast it into the water. But sent a third time, Sir Bedivere took up the sword Excalibur and threw it as far into the water as he could. "There came an arm and a hand above the water and met it, and caught it, and so shook it thrice and brandished, and then vanished away the hand with the sword in the water."

In the first incident, the sword is a sign, and as a sign it works with fateful accuracy. The sword is drawn to be used for the purpose for which it exists; at the same time it serves as a signal to start an event for which swords were made. The irony is strengthened and made universally applicable precisely because the sword is used at once for a purpose for which it was intended and as a signal for which it was chosen. The irony is intolerable because the sign, so uniquely and materially appropriate to its purpose, is misread. (Note also that the snake is symbolic of treachery—is treachery itself—a symbol which explains in part the misreading of the sign.)

In the second incident the sword is used as a symbol. A sign usually has but one meaning to the observer; a symbol may be enriched with several meanings, but in the true symbol all meanings converge to stimulate a unified emotional response in the observer. Though no single meaning is attached to the symbol, still it cannot by its nature represent, for instance, its opposite, as is possible with words. The sword Excalibur stands perhaps for the mysterious and wonderful power of the supernatural world to protect King Arthur; it also suggests that he has been cherished, that he is immortal, and that one day he will return to England when he shall be most needed. In *Le Morte D'Arthur* the sword symbol is used responsibly and communally, and the cluster of feelings that surrounds it may be said to express the ideals of knighthood in the Middle Ages.

We can, if we wish, make anything stand for anything. But wilful and private symbolizing is a risky business, not only because it imperils communication but because it is false to reality. Words, especially highly abstract words, can be twisted to mean the opposite of what we have come to expect them to mean, and we can be wearied out with their contrarieties. But for the most part "object" symbols, even when used in imaginative and uncommonly revealing ways, cannot be changed into something they are not. We may *say* that "war is peace," but we know that a rifle with fixed bayonet is not a white dove with an olive branch, and nothing can convince us that it is, unless, of course, we recognize a deliberate incongruity used for its shock value. We may *say* that "death is life," but we know that the skull of poor Yorick is not the head of a living being. We may *say* that "freedom is slavery," but we may not use the image of a sea gull in full career as an emblem of imprisonment. Plato's choice of a cave as symbolic of the limitations of human understanding was so obviously right as to go without saying; he could not very well have used a tower. It is true that we have attached somewhat arbitrary symbolic meanings to the laurel wreath and to the crown of thorns, but by no stretch of the imagination could we use the crown of sweet laurel to symbolize intense suffering, nor the crown of thorns to symbolize joyous triumph, except insofar as the symbolism may suggest a deeper meaning than the symbol by itself can bear the burden of.

Symbols are more closely linked with reality than are words. We have to *agree* on the meaning of words, because the word is not the thing it stands for but rather a convenient and accepted substitute. The picture symbol, however, is often the thing it stands for, and its power in communication may well be a function of its verisimilitude. Moreover, the symbol is profligate with associations that have accumulated around it, and history is more often than not responsible for the wealth of meaning in a symbol. But ultimately, of course, pictorial symbols, like words, are meaningful only as man has given them meaning, or understands their meaning through the prescriptive connection that they have with his life in the world. Consider for example the cup, reaching as it does far back into antiquity as a symbol. In the Christian faith the cup is heavily weighted with meaning, not least because of its inalienable connection with realities, as in the Last Supper and as the Holy Grail. Nevertheless, the cup is, like the cross, wholly human in meaning.

Man is the measure of all things. And man chooses his symbols according as they are unavoidably linked with his experience as man. We may find in Vitruvius a telling illustration of this idea. In Chapter I of Book IV of his *Ten Books on Architecture*, Vitruvius gives an account (doubtless mythical) of the origins of the three orders and says that when the Ionian colonies of Asia Minor wished to build temples for the immortal gods, they first of all raised a temple to Apollo, such as they had seen in Achaea, "calling it Doric because they had first seen that kind of temple built in the states of the Dorians."

> Wishing to set up columns in that temple, but not having rules for their symmetry, and being in search of some way by which they could render them fit to bear a load and also of a satisfactory beauty of appearance, they measured the imprint of a man's foot and compared this with his height. On finding that, in a man, the foot was one sixth of the height, they applied the same principle to the column, and reared the shaft, including the capital, to a height six times its thickness at its base. Thus the Doric Column, as used in buildings, began to exhibit the proportions, strength, and beauty of the body of a man.

> Just so afterwards, when they desired to construct a temple to Diana in a new style of beauty, they translated these footprints into terms characteristic of the slenderness of women, and thus first made a column the thickness of which was only one eighth of its height, so that it might have a taller look. At the foot they substituted the base in place of a shoe; in the capital they placed the volutes, hanging down at the right and left like curly ringlets, and ornamented its front with cymatia and with festoons of fruit arranged in place of hair, while they brought the flutes down the whole shaft, falling like the folds in the robes worn by matrons. Thus in the invention of the two different kinds of columns, they borrowed manly beauty, naked and unadorned, for the one, and for the other delicacy, adornment, and proportions characteristic of women.

49

> The third order, called Corinthian, is an imitation of the slen-
> derness of a maiden; for the outlines and limbs of maidens, being
> more slender on account of their tender years, admit of prettier
> effects in the way of adornment.

Does the truth inherent in this myth perhaps explain the
reason why the three orders of columns have been so widely
admired? They have an analogy to life, a verisimilitude, a fixed
and basic reference to man himself.

There are other symbols that have been in common use
for centuries, yet they seem never to have lost their power to
evoke an emotional response from the observer. These symbols
came to man as naturally, one might say, taking a thought from
Keats, as "leaves to the tree."

The mother-and-child image is a timeless symbol of this
kind; so also are the images of earth, sky, fire, water, the four
seasons, of certain animals such as horses, of trees, fruit, and
flowers, of light, darkness and of certain colors. These realities
have been used by man from time immemorial as symbols with
which to express his condition. They are a part of him and he
of them.

Very nearly as meaningful as symbols are the works of
man's hands and mind—the harvest, the hearth or dwelling place,
towers, temples, gates, various utensils and weapons, the wheel,
books, machinery and so on. However complicated he may be
or "his works" may become, man still clings to the symbols that
signify for him his daily life in the world. And it is the imaginative use of common symbols that constitutes what we find most
appealing in the visual arts (at least until recent times) and
which leads us irresistibly to them.

The dwelling place, for example, has had a strong appeal
to the artist, as we may judge from the innumerable times it
has been used as a subject in the history of painting. The examples are so numerous, illustrations seem hardly to be called
for—the temples of antiquity as they appear in Pompeian fres-
coes (dwelling places of the gods), walled cities and castles in
mediaeval manuscripts (representing feudalism), the architectural backgrounds of the Renaissance painters (from mangers to
princely palaces), the domestic interiors of the Dutch painters
(the rise of the middle class), the romantic ruins of Piranesi and

Hubert Robert in the eighteenth century, the studios and cafes of the Impressionists, or, to choose a twentieth century example in the United States, the houses and interior scenes of Edward Hopper come to mind as symbolic of a nostalgic and restless mood. The dwelling lends itself to symbolic treatment because it is a real object that speaks unmistakably of man's life and yet may be enormously enriched with associative meaning. The creative imagination finds new and striking correspondences between the dwelling and the life of men, and in the finest works of art there appears a perfection of correspondence between the symbol and what it symbolizes, even though the symbolic performance may be extremely subtle. Edgar Allan Poe's "The Fall of the House of Usher" comes to my mind as a brilliant example of the house used symbolically.

> During the whole of a dull, dark, and soundless day in the autumn of the year, when the clouds hung oppressively low in the heavens, I had been passing alone, on horseback, through a singularly dreary tract of country; and at length found myself, as the shades of evening drew on, within view of the melancholy House of Usher. I know not how it was—but, with the first glimpse of the building, a sense of insufferable gloom pervaded my spirit. . . . I looked upon the scene before me—upon the mere house, and the simple landscape features of the domain—upon the bleak walls— upon the vacant eye-like windows . . . with an utter depression of soul which I can compare to no earthly sensation more properly than to the after-dream of the reveller upon opium—the bitter lapse into everyday life—the hideous dropping off of the veil. . . .

> Shaking off from my spirit what *must* have been a dream, I scanned more narrowly the real aspect of the building. Its principal feature seemed to be that of an excessive antiquity. The discoloration of ages had been great. Minute fungi overspread the whole exterior, hanging in a fine tangled webwork from the eaves. Yet all this was apart from any extraordinary dilapidation. No portion of the masonry had fallen; and there appeared to be a wild inconsistency between its still perfect adaptation of parts and the crumbling condition of the individual stones. . . . Perhaps the eye of a scrutinizing observer might have discovered a barely perceptible fissure, which, extending from the roof of the building in front, made its way down the wall in a zigzag direction, until it became lost in the sullen waters of the tarn.

With incomparable aesthetic sensitivity Poe goes on to work out the similarity between the decaying house and the pathological disintegration of the people within, up to the final simultaneous collapse of both house and the last of the Ushers. The art critic will think of analogous examples in painting, such as the decaying Victorian houses of Burchfield, or a city square by Berman.

In the history of painting, interiors have also been used with symbolic meaning and effect. Call to mind the portrait of George Gisze by Hans Holbein the Younger. Every detail of the painting—vase, carnations, coins, ring-seal, table-rug, documents, quill pens, scales—is strict in its symbolic reference to the life and values of the merchant of the sixteenth century in a commercial and financial center of Europe. And one could say the same of Van Eyck's *Arnolfini portrait* or Clouet's *Diane de Poitiers*.

The window appears also to have held a considerable fascination for painters and writers. It is appealing in its design and purely pictorial possibilities, of course, but in addition, it has a psychological quality about it that invites symbolic use, as in certain paintings of Caspar David Friedrich or Edward Munch. The windows may carry varied meanings for different artists, yet all meanings and interpretations must center upon the looking out on the world or the looking in upon the private life. Keats' image of the window in the "Ode to a Nightingale" is a beautiful symbolic expression of high romance:

> *magic casements, opening on the foam*
> *Of perilous seas, in faery lands forlorn.*

The windows of Matisse are refinements for already cultivated lives looking out upon pleasing vistas of delightful color and pattern. The windows of Edward Hopper look out upon a changing world, or they stare, like forgotten people, absentmindedly into space, or they look in upon loneliness. And a realistic window of Andrew Wyeth, curtain fluttering, speaks of strange aspects of the life within.

The tree has been used as a symbol of life and immortality by very nearly all peoples. It seems to have appealed spontaneously to the imagination of man as an image that he could use to express his own feeling for death and resurrection; and it has been a favorite subject in literature and the visual arts for a very long time. The pine was sacred to Dionysos, and the conifer to Osiris. The Christmas tree is still a vivid symbol of the gift of everlasting life. "Among the Chinese the Tree of Life was believed to be a very wonderful *persica* or *peachtree* situated in the Happy Islands of the Eastern Ocean"; and the Egyptians supposed that "In the East of Heaven stands that high *Sycamore*-tree upon which the gods sit, the tree of life by which they live."[1] In contemporary literature there is Truman Capote's "luxurious" tree (in *The Grass Harp*), "more airy than dense; its leaves, rust and speckled, green and greenish gold, ... rippling like the colors on a peacock's tail." This tree, too, is a kind of tree-of-life for those who build their tree-house in it and seek to live free and happy in their freedom.

The symbol has within its form and being the meaning it is intended to convey. The meaning attached to the object symbol is not arbitrary, nor has it come about merely through long association with what it stands for, so as to be, as it were, a cultural habit. On the contrary, in true symbolic expression there is a transcendental parity, a spontaneous and irresistible correspondence between the concrete image and the thing it stands for. If one wishes, he may think of symbols as primordial images of the collective unconscious, taking the idea from the psychology of Jung. But one may not have to plumb that deeply. It may be enough to observe that "man is the measure," and that such symbols as speak to him bear an intimate and undeniable connection with his humanity. The parity between the "thing" and the "thought" is transcendental in the sense that it cannot be otherwise, except as human sanity shall be imperiled. And it is the genius of great artists and writers that they have seen these transcendental parities intuitively and expressed them powerfully.

When Othello, determined to kill Desdemona, looks at the lamp burning by her bed and says, "Put out the light, and then put out the light," Shakespeare puts into his mouth symbolic utterance so right, so exact, as to be incontrovertible. The similarity between light and life, for man, is categorical and inevitable.

---

[1]Harold Bayley, *The Lost Language of Symbolism*, (Philadelphia, 1913), Vol II, p. 269f.

Out of this train of thought may we possibly arrive at a new way of discussing the long-standing conflict between abstract and representational painting? What is the role of symbol in contemporary abstract art? Some critics have talked about painting before the twentieth century as "representational," saying that its intention is to depict objects which we recognize, that it is "realistic," that it is two-dimensional representation of three dimensional objects. "During the nineteenth century artists . . . let the work consist almost entirely in a fiction of human realities." Now this is not altogether sound criticism, much as one must admire Jose Ortega y Gasset's essay on "The Dehumanization of Art." More often than not, the great painters have "reproduced" objects not so much that we shall merely recognize them, but so that they have become symbols. As if Masaccio or Botticelli or Velazquez or Goya were merely representational painters! I think of the popular *Don Manuel Osorio* (the Boy with Cats and Birds) by Goya. Who would say that these cats and birds are nothing more than two-dimensional representations of three-dimensional objects? What distinguishes the painting, beyond its brilliant color and technical execution, is the haunting quality of its symbolism. The birds in the cage, the bird on the string, the relationship of the cats to the birds in the painting and of cats and birds in everyday life, all these are symbolic of dramatic conflict held in suspension, of tension unresolved—in this painting forever. With the same instinctive sense for symbolic surety of meaning yet with a purpose of conveying a quite different message, Edward Hicks, the American primitive of the nineteenth century, created a wonderfully moving scene in his *The Peaceable Kingdom.* Here the leopard is lying down with the lamb, and the white man is meeting peacefully with the Indian. As in the Goya painting, the meaning is unmistakable, and the parity between object and idea is not only self-evident but is rendered with extraordinary emotional clarity.

The painting of the post-impressionists, of Cezanne, Gauguin, and Van Gogh, is gradually acquiring symbolic significance, as new relationships and meaning are discovered in their works; and one can begin to see a similar adjustment in our understanding of Cubism and other cultural movements of the early twentieth century. But much of the recent and current abstract painting seems to present a new problem. Though often delighting the eye and satisfying the pattern-making request of the mind (and in that sense comforting), sometimes touching the spectator's emotional life deeply, a purely abstract painting is by and large symbolically "non-communicative," unless and until our changing perceptions discover that arrangements and relationships of lines and shapes and colors may in themselves speak of human ideas and emotions. It is here, of course, that the embarrassment lies for the untutored spectator. For if they *are* communicative, what *do* these shapes and visual textures say? I recall having read somewhere an observation of W. H. Auden's that "a new convention is a revolution in sensibility." With even a modest measure of modern sensibility, it should be possible for one to look at an abstract painting as an event in itself, an object new in the world, not standing for anything except itself. And as a new event it may be a genuine addition to visual experience. Or an abstract painting may be viewed as a complicated emotion in itself, like a fine piece of bravura acting in the theatre where for the moment we do not attend to the denotative meaning of the words. The painting (perhaps even the making of the painting) is, as it were, a performance to be admired for itself. At a symposium held in 1951 at the Museum of Modern Art where six American artists discussed "What Abstract Art Means to Me," George L. K. Morris said, "Our problems may not be new to art, but the conception of an abstract picture as we know it, certainly *is*. Can you imagine it in any other time— an artist just putting shapes together—shapes that represent nothing, either alone or in combination? He puts a frame around it, and offers it on the open market, just as a good thing to have around and look at; something that will speak to you as an independent personality, and yet is very quiet." This is a sound aesthetic, but it does not go far enough. A somewhat more revealing way of talking about abstract painting is to be found in a probing article by Harold Rosenberg in *Art News* (December, 1952).

The new American painting is not "pure art," since the extrusion of the object was not for the sake of the aesthetic. The apples weren't brushed off the table in order to make room for perfect relations of space and color. They had to go so that nothing would get in the way of the act of painting. In this gesturing with materials the aesthetic, too, has been subordinated. Form, color, composition, drawing, are auxiliaries, any one of which—or practically all, as has been attempted, logically, with unpainted canvases—can be dispensed with. What matters always is the revelation contained in the act. It is to be taken for granted that in the final effect, the image, whatever be or be not in it, will be a *tension*.

When all is said, however, there remains the stubborn thought that all works of man's imagination are a kind of conversation between the maker and the spectator; and it is hard to believe that any work of art can be without "meaning" of one kind or another, meaning with reference to a body of accepted beliefs or to cultural habits, or meaning in the sense of being a graphic representation of the modern sensibility. In abstract painting the process of symbolization, that is, of conversation, has a new and different relation to the common reservoir of experience and at times seems *not* to have evolved out of the mass experience of humanity—thus, although there seems not to be that inevitability of parity between a recognizable object and the thought or feeling for which it stands, still it is unthinkable that symbolic expression of one kind or another is not taking place. Tentatively, then, we may put forth the proposition that although abstract painting is "non-representational" and therefore non-symbolic in the communal sense (that it is rather more like music than literature), it is still a pictorial expression of the inner life of modern man. The iconography is more than personal and private; some inner excitement is being talked about on the canvas, and some innuendo, some hint, some inkling of the painter's feeling is present, integrated with life in the twentieth century and expressing with subtle verisimilitude the character of our age—the tension, the anxiety, the rejections, the search for spiritual clarity, the quest for freedom.

A Mondrian expresses himself in one way, a Leger in quite another, and among modern American abstract-expressionists a Kline, a Motherwell, a Baziotes in still other ways; yet all works of art reflect in some fashion their social and intellectual milieu

56

through a choice of imagery which records the perception common to the age. In the case of the modern painter, the symbolic parity lies in the lines and shapes and colors so composed as to make an emotional comment on the condition of the painter himself, how it is with him, in the twentieth century.

Five Metaphors from the Modern Repertory

W HEN WE WISH to say something about ourselves or our environment, we choose a *way* of ordering our thoughts, a way that will be, we hope, meaningful to ourselves and to our listeners, a way that will do justice to the eager activity of our minds. Metaphor appears to be a very effective way of making meaning, if we may judge from the extensive and successful use of it by poets. Yet metaphor consists of something more than airy nothing. Rather, it "gives to airy nothing / A local habitation and a name." One part of the metaphor exists in everyday reality, the transitory portion, while the other part, the enduring portion, is a thought, an intuition, an airy nothing. When we join the transitory image with the enduring thought, we create a metaphor, a way of uttering an insight about ourselves and our world.

I. THE PRISON

The transitory portion of a metaphor is often selected from among prevailing images of one's time, from among those particulars which affect us emotionally and impress people of the time as having unusual power and meaning. For example, the prison has been a powerful reality in many societies, and notable works of literature and art have employed the image of the prison to give substance to a thought or feeling. It must have been very real and powerful to Plato, and he chose it more than once as the perfect apt transitory portion of the metaphor he creates to express the philosophy of idealism. In the *Phaedo* Socrates says, "Those too who have been preeminent for holiness of life are released from this earthly prison, and go to their pure home which is above, and dwell in the purer earth." The allegory of the cave is also based on the prison metaphor, its enduring portion the ascent of the soul out of the cave or prison of human imperfection and misery into intellectual freedom where all things beautiful and right are seen in the light of a great vision.

The prison or dungeon was a bitter reality in the eighteenth and nineteenth centuries and appears often in the works of European writers and artists of the time. There were, for example, the engravings of Giovanni Battista Piranesi, Beethoven's *Fidelio,* Dumas' *The Count of Monte Cristo,* Victor Hugo's *Les Miserables,* and of course that symbol of all prisons of all time, the Bastille.

In the works of the English romantic poets the prison metaphor continued to assist tellingly in the revelations of Platonic idealism.[1] For Blake "A robin redbreast in a cage / Puts all heaven in a rage"; after the death of his brothers, the prisoner of Chillon in Byron's poem says, "And the whole earth would henceforth be / A wider prison unto me"; the fireside is a prison to Wordsworth when he is melancholy, a prison from which he is released only by the glad song of the thrush. But of the metaphors of the English romantic poets the one that comes first to mind is found in Wordsworth's "Ode on the Intimations of Immortality":

Our birth is but a sleep and a forgetting
The Soul that rises with us, our life's Star,
    Hath had elsewhere its setting,
      And cometh from afar:
    Not in entire forgetfulness,
    And not in utter nakedness,
But trailing clouds of glory do we come
      From God, who is our home:
    Heaven lies about us in our infancy!
Shades of the prison-house begin to close
      Upon the growing Boy,
But he beholds the light and whence it flows,
      He sees it in his joy;
The Youth, who daily farther from the east
      Must travel, still is Nature's priest,

---

[1]One wonders what images a Platonist *could* use if there were no prisons in his society and he had no knowledge of "stone walls and iron bars." On the other hand it is interesting to ask whether some intuition of confinement in the world has not perhaps given men the idea of a similar incarceration in a man-made jail for purposes of worldly punishment. Opposed to the prison in the imagination of man are the heavens—home of that romantic symbol of perfect freedom, the skylark—even the hills, age-old images of emancipation from the fetters and restraints of the earthbound.

And by the vision splendid
Is on his way attended;
At length the Man perceives it die away,
And fade into the light of common day.

The prison image is a pervading fantasy in western literature. Inspired by a theme from Dante's Inferno, Eliot brings the metaphor of the prison into the twentieth century when in *The Waste Land* the protagonist of that poem watches the crowd of people flowing over London Bridge and says, "I had not thought death had undone so many." Indeed, this passage in the poem suggests a similarity between crowds of people moving in a city and convicts moving in a prison yard: "Sighs, short and infrequent, were exhaled, / And each man fixed his eyes before his feet." The representation of the world as a vast purgatorial prison has persevered for more than two thousand years, and it is revealing that one of the most celebrated of modern poems should revive the idea that life in this world is death, a death from which one may be delivered only through the mystery of spiritual rebirth. In the last section of *The Waste Land* Eliot uses the metaphor again in a somewhat more modern interpretation. Following the voice of thunder and the exhortation to sympathy, the poem expresses human loneliness and isolation in the modern world through the image of the prison— "each in his prison / Thinking of the key"—of the key of sympathy which will open the door and release us from the bondage of our selfishness.[2]

As the philosophers of the seventeenth century observed, so long as men live in society they will have to give up some of their freedoms to the social contract. Laws and restraints are inevitable in any social order, and images of the prison will

---

[2]Compare the prison metaphors in W. H. Auden's poem, "In Memory of W. B. Yeats." ("And each in the cell of himself is almost convinced of his freedom.") One of the most anguished cries in modern literature is this aphorism from Franz Kafka's "Notes from the Year 1920": "He feels imprisoned on this earth, he feels constricted; the melancholy, the impotence, the sickness, the feverish fancies of the captive afflict him; no comfort can comfort him, since it is merely comfort, gentle head-splitting comfort glazing the brutal fact of imprisonment. But if he is asked what he actually wants he cannot reply, for—that is one of his strongest proofs—he has no conception of freedom." (From *The Great Wall of China* [New York, 1946], p. 265.)

occur in literature to express the *feeling* of restriction—in some ages and societies strong, as in our own, perhaps because of the density of modern bureaucratic organization, in some weak or non-existent. The image also expresses the feeling of immense loneliness, a characteristic feeling, apparently, of our time.

We meet the prison metaphor in full modern dress in Jean-Paul Sartre's *No Exit*. However much one may wish to fly away, however one may delude himself into thinking he is free as a skylark, in sober moments, we suspect we are most subtly "trapped," that there is no escape from this small room, the world, in which we are doomed to live with other people.[3] Hell is not fire and brimstone and red-hot pokers, says Garcin in *No Exit*. "Hell is—other people!" Metaphorically, then, we are imprisoned in the world and compelled to live out our lives suffering from the wounds inflicted by other people. *No Exit* brings up to date the mutual hatred and repulsion of the traitors in Dante's lowest circle of Hell. The metaphor of "no exit" appears aptly chosen as a modern expression of the *feeling* of incarceration, especially since the transitory portion of the metaphor is drawn from the image of the enclosed theatre or multiple dwelling which purposely holds a number of people. To be captive in a small space with other people in a state of panic with no exit is indeed to suffer greatly at their hands.[4]

If we were *alone* in the world, we should be truly free—we are inclined to think. But we are not alone in the world, and for Sartre, the only realistic freedom is acceptance of full re-

---

[3] Our persistent, impassioned desire to get to the moon may well be a strategy by which we hope to circumvent the sentence of imprisonment in the world, especially since the world's room is shrinking daily in apparent size. Sails on the horizon were once thought of as images of freedom; the astronaut cruising through the illimitable in his spacecraft may become a modern image of freedom, though his vehicle suggests a more severe confinement than the erstwhile sailing vessel, open as it was to the then wide world. Even in the swift airliners of today one has the feeling of being in captivity, literally strapped in, far more than one has when he is traveling on a train or boat.

[4] The image of the "wall" as barrier—often as death—is vivid and meaningful in the twentieth century and is used by poets and writers from Robert Frost through Sartre and John Hersey, and with luminous irony in Kafka's *The Great Wall of China*.

sponsibility for our behavior.[5] For the most part we tend to think of freedom today as the opportunity for the uninhibited expression of our own individuality, largely through freedom of movement. When, then, we discover the NO EXIT sign lit by day and night for our information, we tend to despair; for to many people in the modern world it sometimes *seems* as though there were "no way out," unless perhaps through the now not so illimitable space to the stars above.

Walls, prisons, guards, keys, the trial, the conviction, the sentence, the shutting of the door, the confinement, and the escape—all the realities and fantasies of imprisonment occur so frequently in Western World literature there can scarcely be any doubt that the prison image describes with emotional intensity the feelings and thoughts which people have about freedom, not necessarily freedom from the literal jail but the nature of freedom itself, what it is for, how to define it. The metaphysical contrarieties in the thought of our time are not better illustrated than in this aphorism from Kafka's "Notes":

---

[5]Walter Kaufmann in his *The Faith of a Heretic* (Garden City, New York, 1961) has dealt severely with the confusions that surround the concept of commitment as interpreted by the existentialists. As a man of reason he feels that commitment is often very unreasonable, fanaticism in effect, and that much that was unholy has been done in its name. His commentary on Kierkegaard's concept of faith may not be quite just, however. The story of Abraham and Isaac should, perhaps, be read as a parable, that is, a metaphor, an exaggerated way of thinking about or describing "faith," a powerful transitory image of the *idea* of faith, not to be taken literally but imaginatively as expressive of the burning desire of all men to believe, to trust. The compelling *wish* to believe and the enduring hope that the good will come true in spite of commanding appearances to the contrary are existential facts of human experience.

At times the romantic poets were unexpectedly sophisticated in their interpretation of imprisonment, recognizing necessity and consenting, even eagerly, to earthly bondage, turning it to account as a fact not without use and value. For the prisoner of Chillon, the prison becomes a "second home," a "hermitage" for the solitary soul, a place of refuge. In Wordsworth's sonnet "Nuns Fret Not At Their Convent's Narrow Room" the poet says that for those "Who have felt the weight of too much liberty," the prison unto which they doom themselves "no prison is," as with the nuns who fret not at their convent's narrow room, the hermit who is contented with his cell, the student in his citadel, the weaver at his loom, the bee in the foxglove bell, and the poet bound "Within the Sonnet's scanty plot of ground."

He could have resigned himself to a prison. To end as a prisoner—
that could be a life's ambition. But it was a barred cage that he
was in. Calmly and insolently, as if at home, the din of the world
streamed out and in through the bars, the prisoner was really free,
he could take part in everything, nothing that went on outside
escaped him, he could simply have left the cage, the bars were
yards apart, he was not even a prisoner.[6]

II. The Wasteland

In literature, probably the most widely known metaphor of
our time is the metaphor of the "wasteland" from the poem by
T. S. Eliot. When *The Waste Land* was first published in 1922,
general critical judgment pronounced it so ridiculously complex
and recondite as to be unreadable. But the genius of T. S. Eliot
and the relevance of his poem to the condition of the modern
world have since become evident and celebrated. Eliot appears
to be one of those writers whom literary historians select as the
genius speaking for his age.

Eliot's intuitive understanding of the world of his time coincides with the silent feelings of his contemporaries; and he
articulates their mood in the compressed and impassioned language of poetry. Or better, the poet identifies the malaise and
gives it meaning through a symbol or image that turns out to
be wholly acceptable.

However, when an all-encompassing image enters the public
domain, it is usually accompanied by a considerable retinue of
literary and historical servants. The mythic image of a wasteland
that is found in the legends of the Sangraal and the Arthurian
stories gives a local habitation and a name to the idea of spiritual
aridity. And the pilgrimage or quest, the seeking out of that

---

[6]*Op. cit.*, p. 264. Compare the following from "Spiritual Autobiography" by Simone Weil: "I fell in love with Saint Francis of Assisi as soon
as I came to know him. I always believed and hoped that one day Fate
would force upon me the condition of a vagabond and a beggar which he
embraced freely. Actually I felt the same way about prison." Like Kafka,
Simone Weil longs for a condition that is positive (even if it has to be
the lowest—categorical, perhaps, because it is the lowest), a well-marked
condition, explicit, and not, as it were, an ambiguous condition of being
half in and half out. (From *Waiting for God* by Simone Weil [New York,
1951], p. 65.)

which is concealed, the search for the Holy Grail, the search for salvation, appears to be a basic fact of existence.

The master metaphor of the Middle Ages is the pilgrimage as a quest for salvation, the literal journey, perhaps, to the holy place, or simply everyman's journey, his going forth toward an unknown destination in search of a mysterious something not revealed to him. The pilgrim knows only that he must seek and continue to seek with single-minded purpose until, if he is devout and faithful, he is vouchsafed the reason for his journey in the beatific vision which is the consummation of all his wandering and questing. The metaphor of the pilgrimage or journey is found in the Arthurian legends in the search for the Holy Grail, is expressed with great beauty in *Sir Gawain and the Green Knight*, is the religious motive of the historical Crusades, and is the artless natural framework of *The Canterbury Tales*.

In *The Waste Land*, Eliot concentrates on the decay of the modern world, on its wasteland character, on the spiritual aridity of our times rather than on the image of the journey or pilgrimage. Indeed, it is because the will is atrophied, because spiritual purpose is infirm and hesitant that no quest is undertaken in the twentieth century. The emphasis in the poem is on the lack of spiritual determination, on the spiritual sickness of our time.

Though he does not use the term "wasteland" in the descriptive passage which opens Chapter II of *The Great Gatsby* (1925), F. Scott Fitzgerald may well have had T. S. Eliot's famous image in mind when he wrote the following:

> About half way between West Egg and New York the motor road hastily joins the railroad and runs beside it for a quarter of a mile, so as to shrink away from a certain desolate area of land. This is a valley of ashes—a fantastic farm where ashes grow like wheat into ridges and hills and grotesque gardens: where ashes take the forms of houses and chimneys and rising smoke and, finally, with a transcendent effort, of ash-gray men who move dimly and already crumbling through the powdery air. Occasionally a line of gray cars crawls along an invisible track, gives out a ghastly creak, and comes to rest, and immediately the ash-gray men swarm up with leaden spades and stir up an impenetrable cloud, which screens their obscure operations from your sight.

> But above the gray land and the spasms of bleak dust which drift endlessly over it, you perceive, after a moment, the eyes of Doctor T. J. Eckleberg. The eyes of Doctor T. J. Eckleberg are

blue and gigantic—their retinas are one yard high. They look out of no face, but, instead, from a pair of enormous yellow spectacles which pass over a non-existent nose. Evidently some wild wag of an oculist set them there to fatten his practice in the borough of Queens, and then sank down himself into eternal blindness, or forgot them and moved away. But his eyes, dimmed a little by many paintless days, under sun and rain, brood on over the solemn dumping ground.[7]

The brooding Dr. Eckleburg is, perhaps, Fitzgerald's depiction of the legendary sick Fisher King who plays so large a role in *The Waste Land*.

The image of the modern world as a spiritual wasteland now appears to be an apt and fitting figure. Though the social revolution of the 1930's sought to repudiate the wasteland metaphor and to replace it with images of fertility and the fellowship of the common man, the desolation caused by World War II gave a new rightness to the "wasteland" analogy. In any event, Eliot's metaphor has prevailed for more than forty years as a literary description of an anarchic and spiritually desiccated modern world.

III. THE MONSTER

Though human beings in society may have little control, individually, over their predicament (existing in the world *and* in society), each thinks of himself *as* something—a "human being," for instance. What, then, is a human being. Everyone knows what a human being is, or at least what a human being is not. A human being is *not* an insect—there are demonstrable differences. But a human being may be said to be *like* an insect. Even if we do not know what we *are*, we may say we know what we are *like;* and it is what we say we are like that makes all the difference in our attitude toward ourselves and our neighbors. Man is like a machine. Man is like an angel. Man is like an insect. Man is a rhinoceros. Man is a trapped animal. Man is garbage.

In Franz Kafka's celebrated short story *Metamorphosis,* Gregor Samsa, the central character, thinks of himself as an enor-

---

[7]This selection is taken from the volume entitled *The Last Tycoon,* which includes *The Great Gatsby* (New York, 1941).

mous insect, repulsive, disgusting. Although here and there in the history of European literature authors have pointed sharply to the similarity between some of their characters and vicious or contemptible animal creatures, their purpose was to show explicitly the ample distance between noble human beings and, say, despicable quadrupeds. The comparison was made for the purpose of elevating the human. But much of modern literature seems intent upon identifying the human with the beastly. It is doubtful that even Swift thought of human beings as in a class with baboons. He made it perfectly clear that in his estimation his friends were not yahoos. But the swine in George Orwell's *Animal Farm* bear a striking resemblance to all human beings whether they are one's friends or one's enemies. Indeed, at the end of the story, while the farm animals gazed upon their animal leaders (pigs) and their human neighbors, they saw that something had happened to the faces of the pigs. "The creatures outside looked from pig to man and from man to pig, and from pig to man again; but already it was impossible to say which was which."[8]

The image of man as a "human being" was given its modern definition during the Renaissance. This is the image we have in mind when we deplore the non-humanistic trends of our time. Clinging to this image, we are sickened by the appalling idea that we may not be "human" at all, but enormous insects or brainy pigs. In general we still *say* that man is Renaissance man. But what appears to trouble our sleep is the suspicion that the Renaissance ideal was only another piece of self-delusion and that man is really, at best, a "despicable biped" and at worst a pig, an enormous insect, or a field creature (as in Kafka's "The Burrow") pitifully erecting his flimsy defenses against an unseen and unnameable enemy, consumed by a very understandable

---

[8]George Orwell, *Animal Farm* (New York, 1946), p. 118. Eugene O'Neill writes allegorically about the emotional clashes consequent upon the ambiguities in the human predicament. In *The Hairy Ape* (1922), the main character, Yank, is described in the beginning as having the appearance of "Neanderthal Man," not quite man and not quite gorilla; and the irony of the last scene is unrelieved as the caged Gorilla of the Zoo crushes Yank "in a murderous hug," throws the dying man's body in the cage, and shuts the door. *"Perhaps,"* says O'Neill in the last words of the play, *"Perhaps, the Hairy Ape at last belongs."*

anxiety. Shakespeare's Dogberry is a monument of majesty compared to Gregor Samsa.

The image of man created by the Renaissance centered upon the concepts of personality and character. These are exalted ideas and are subsumed under the master concept of the richly endowed individuality. The dignity of man derives from the integrity that is his and that is expressed through his unique personality and through his self-discipline that we recognize as character. He is a special creature singled out for glory. This image of man is not, of course, new with the Renaissance; indeed, it is very ancient, a characteristic of pagan as well as of Christian beliefs. Man in his fullness is a nature, that is, a human nature, or better, a human spirit, an ideal form, a central beautiful form against the prepared and ideal form of the landscape, against a framed space which dotes upon and admires its lovely human figures, a madonna in a painting by Raphael, a David in a sculpture by Michelangelo.

The new image of man as portrayed by several distinguished contemporary painters and sculptors is forcefully presented in a single text by Peter Selz in *New Images of Man,* published by the Museum of Modern Art in connection with its exhibition "New Images of Man" in 1959. There can be no doubt of the range and creative power of the new imagination. These figures cast in bronze or painted on canvas distinctly *resemble* human beings, but seldom human beings as we are accustomed to seeing them. They are powerful impressions of the mood of modern man, plastic evocations of the way he feels. Rather than recognizable as everyday persons, they are self-conscious figures, evolving *out* of their "human" form into another form, tormented and suffering in the contemplation of their own new image.

Writing about the sculpture of Kenneth Armitage, Selz says: "Like Gregor in Kafka's *Metamorphosis,* these human figures with their thin extremities are turned into helpless bugs." Of the sculpture of Reg Butler, Selz observes that his sculpture "always relates to the human figure," but resembles "bird and insect forms." Jean Dubuffet's painting *Woman with Furs* "is a conglomeration of lichens or organisms seen under a microscope." Willem de Kooning's *Woman I* has the look of a predatory beast, enfanged, lusting after prey with single-minded intensity. (There is something to be said for the modern artist's verisimilitude. At least we often come to see people as the modern artist shows them to us.) "After the initial shock of her appearance wears off," says the art critic Thomas B. Hess of the de Kooning Woman, "she sits next to us on a bus, or is seen waving at someone behind us in a restaurant."[9]

Man has been called a variety of names in the history of the Western World—a creature like unto the Olympian gods, a political animal, a rational being, the temple of the Holy Spirit. At the moment he is sometimes seen as a human monster, less companionable than the legendary wivern of heraldy. In *New Images of Man*, he is a prodigy of distortion, by turns sinister and pathetic, threatening and corroded with decay.[10]

Yet there is method in this madness. Dwelling as so many sculptors and painters do on the "despoiled and debauched" image of the human figure, they still believe, I suspect, with Leonard Baskin that "The forging of works of art is one of man's remaining semblances to divinity." These ogres, in addition to having their own personalities, are reflections of a modern state of mind, a state of mind characterized by repulsion and by longing. Self-conscious before the "cracked mirror" of the world, these figures are waiting to be born again into something they can at least understand and accept. As Paul Tillich says in his Prefatory Note to *New Images of Man*, if there is anxiety and despair, there is also longing and hope, "a reaching out into the unknown."

IV. THE MACHINE

Though at first glance it might seem that the machine metaphor is a common form of expression today, it is no longer, I believe, taken seriously as revelation of the human condition in the second half of the twentieth century. But from the late

---

[9]Thomas B. Hess, *Willem de Kooning* (New York, 1959), p. 29.

[10]In Samuel Beckett's play *Endgame*, a moving tragic drama of the human condition in the modern world, two of the characters, an old man and an old woman, appear to "live" in garbage cans. Their names are Nagg and Nell.

eighteenth century until, one might say, Chaplin's film *Modern Times* in 1936, the machine idea exercised a potent influence over the human mind. There was, for example, the all-encompassing image in the eighteenth century of the universe as a vast clock running according to unalterable mechanical law; and in 1820 Napoleon Bonaparte could say with conviction, "We are a machine made to live. . . . Our body is a watch, intended to go for a given time." Dickens speaks of "this machine called Man!" and someone referred to Daniel Webster as "a steam-engine in trousers." Karl Marx in *Capital* condemns "the intellectual desolation artificially produced by converting immature human beings into mere machines," and Havelock Ellis, later in the nineteenth century, was convinced that the "greatest task before civilization at present is to make machines what they ought to be, the slaves, instead of the masters of men." In 1922, when T. S. Eliot described in *The Waste Land* the "human engine" waiting "Like a taxi throbbing waiting," there was still considerable vitality in the image, but when, in 1938, Sartre's hero, Roquentin, in *Nausea* feels his body "at rest like a precision machine," the meaning in the similarity has diminished very nearly, I think, to the status of cliche.

In his famous chapter "The Dynamo and the Virgin" in *The Education of Henry Adams,* Henry Adams presented the dynamo as the greatest force in the Western World, standing for power, inexorable law, organization, productivity (if not fertility). Yet "All the steam in the world," he said, "could not, like the Virgin, build Chartres." Instead, together with the dynamo, it was steam that built the modern world, whatever opinion one may have of either. Modern metaphorical use of the machine is found in Eugene O'Neill's *Dynamo* (New York, 1929) in which the dynamo is represented in the mind of the protagonist as the "Divine Image on earth" of the "Great Mother of Eternal Life, Electricity." "Her power houses are the new churches!" It may very well have been that O'Neill was inspired by Adams' "The Dynamo and the Virgin." In any event, it is interesting to read in that chapter that "Everyone, even among Puritans, knew that neither Diana of the Ephesians nor any of the Oriental goddesses was worshipped for her beauty. She was goddess because of her

69

force; she was the animated dynamo; she was reproduction—the greatest and most mysterious of all energies; all she needed was to be fecund." For comparison, it is instructive to quote from one of the stage directions in O'Neill's *Dynamo:* "The oil switches, with their spindly steel legs, their square, criss-crossed steel bodies (the containers inside looking like bellies), their six cupped arms stretching upward, seem like queer Hindu idols tortured into scientific supplications."[11]

The urge to create a "mechanical" man has challenged the imagination since Mary Shelley's *Frankenstein* was published in 1817. *R.U.R.*, for instance, by Karel Capek, first produced in Prague in 1920, is the story of the robot who becomes master over man but cannot survive because he lacks life and soul. For the most part, the use of the image of the mechanical man in modern literature has been humanistic, that is to say, critical of the thought that man is nothing but a machine or a cog in a machine, and Chaplin's *Modern Times* was a powerful satire on the idea of man as machine, suggesting distinctly and in characteristic Chaplinesque style that human beings are human *individuals* and should not be regimented by the world of machines. The machine is the machine and Charlie Chaplin is the man, and the two are quite different.

But as I observed at the outset of this section, the machine metaphor appears to have lost its vigor of expression in the literature of today. The computing machine is said to be "like" the human brain, but the metaphor is not emotionally significant, and a statement of the following kind appeals to us as rather more amusing than instructive:

The normal healthy brain puts out "remarkable mileage." It consumes 1 teaspoon of sugar per hour. Using the terminology of industry, total operating costs are remarkably low. Energy output per hour is equal to that of a 20-watt light bulb. It is remarkable that while the combined brain energy of the group of men who worked on the atomic bomb did not equal the electrical energy consumed by the lights in an average office, nevertheless, they released atomic energy which is now being measured in megatons.

[11]Act III, Scene 2.

Thus the brain is the control organ that directs the power flow of modern industry.[12]

If the metaphor of the machine stirs our feelings at all today, it would seem to be in terms of the sick machine, or the machine destroying itself, as in objects created by the sculptor, Jean Tinguely. But again, in these displays, the effect, if not the intention, is apparently more comic than tragic.[13]

V. THE HOSPITAL

Although Freud warned against graphic representations of psychoanalytical hypotheses, it is meaningful that the "unconscious" should have lent itself so readily to interpretation in the popular imagination as a secret subterranean "place" where repressed wishes are kept in captivity, a dungeon for unruly and wicked thoughts. Naturally, the sole aim of the repressed desire or impulse is freedom, and on occasions, at night, like the ghost of Hamlet's father, it is allowed (under surveillance of the censor and clad in suitable ghostly garments) to venture into the upper world and there unfold its tale, though forbidden to tell *all* "the secrets of the prison-house." But by the middle of the twentieth century the Freudian theories came to be expressed more in terms of the "hospital" than of the prison, and the "unconscious" becomes the place of "sick" rather than of wicked or criminal thoughts, even a place of refuge from the brutalities of the world.

Though there are many philosophies offered for our inspection in the modern world, one is conspicuous by its absence. There appears to be no positive Philosophy of Health. One remembers that in ages past there were, for instance, the ideals of the healthy mind in a healthy body, and earlier, in classical antiquity, of the beautiful mind in a beautiful body. Though scarcely an ideal, today's philosophy of health appears ironically often to be the notion that modern man is a sick mind in a sick

---

[12]From "The Management Team—Its Selection and Development" by Robert K. Burns, in the *Year Book* of the American Iron and Steel Institute (New York, 1955).

[13]There is probably some relation today between the machine metaphor and "junk" sculpture where iron monsters display strong evidence of suffering under the burden of their existence; and it must be said that some pieces are emotionally very moving.

body. Witness the multitude of "sick" jokes, the statistical evidence of widespread mental illness, and the continuous building of new and larger hospitals everywhere. An amusing cartoon which I saw recently, but unfortunately cannot document, pictures two heavily bearded young men standing on a city street observing a third heavily bearded young man walking past them with his head down upon his chest in a mood of despair. One of the observers says in evident disgust as he watches the passerby, "What bugs me is this sicker-than-thou attitude."

Popular expressions of the "sick" modern might be merely comic correctives to too much faddish despair and sophomoric melancholy. We could let it go at that except for the deeper evidence of "sickness" which is to be found in many first-rate pieces of contemporary imaginative literature.

What *is* sickness? The question is in a sense unanswerable unless one has a positive philosophy of health. Such a philosophy was on the way to being built in the 1930s. "A quart of milk every day on every doorstep" was a vigorous popular image; but the forces inimical to man of the twentieth century swept like a tidal wave over the concept of green pastures and still waters. I should like in this essay to present only those metaphors which seem especially meaningful in what they say about the modern world; and I find that the metaphor of the "hospital" is widespread and apparently one of the most acceptable. So far as I know, the metaphor of the world-as-a-hospital was first used in the modern sense by Baudelaire.[14] The prose poem "Anywhere Out of the World" opens with these lines:

> Life is a Hospital, in which every patient is possessed by the desire to change his bed. This one would prefer to suffer in front of the stove and that one believes he would get well if he were placed by the window.

In the poem "Reversibility" Baudelaire calls upon the angels of gaiety, goodness, health, beauty, joy and asks each if they have known their opposite:

---

[14]The quotations from Baudelaire are taken from *Baudelaire, Rimbaud, Verlaine, Selected Verse and Prose Poems*, ed. Joseph Bernstein, trans. Arthur Symons (New York, 1947).

Angel full of health, have you known the Fevers,
That along the walls of hospitals go sagging,
Like exiles who seek the sun, find hell's retrievers,
Who move their lips, foot after tired foot dragging?
Angel full of health, have you known the Fevers?

In his introduction to *Baudelaire, Rimbaud, Verlaine,* Joseph M. Bernstein observes that when we ask about Baudelaire's greatness, we insist on stressing his modernity, "his direct and unusually vibrant appeal to modern man." And it is, I think, in Baudelaire's preoccupation with "sickness" that his modernity lies, in his anticipation of the anguish of modern man, "a divided man often at odds with himself and with life." In any event, the hospital metaphor has persevered into the literature of our time, and, as one might suspect, forcefully in some of the poems of T. S. Eliot. There is, for example, the variation on the theme in "The Love Song of J. Alfred Prufrock" in the first three lines:

Let us go then, you and I,
When the evening is spread out against the sky
Like a patient etherised upon a table.

The metaphor is used more explicitly in *Four Quartets* in the poem "East Coker" where section IV is developed almost entirely in terms of sickness—in the first stanza the use of "surgeon," in the second "nurse," in the third "The whole earth is our hospital," in the fourth "chill" and "fever," in the fifth the irony of our delusion that we like to think, in spite of the spiritual malaise, "That we are sound, substantial flesh and blood."

It is in the plays of Tennessee Williams that the sickness metaphors come prominently before the contemporary audience. In *A Streetcar Named Desire* the theme of sickness is vivified by the appearance of the "strangers," the doctor and the nurse, who come for Blanche to take her away to the place of sanctuary, the hospital. The strangers enter the play like "gods out of the machine," and Blanche, in one of the most pathetic lines in the modern theatre, appeals to their mercy saying, "I have always depended on the kindness of strangers." There is scarcely a play of Williams' which does not have as its major theme the theme of sickness both physical and mental, but in *Period of Adjustment* the world as hospital is given an optimistic turn when the

73

unhappy newlywed Isabel, who is a nurse, comforts her husband, who suffers from nervous "shakes."

> Inside or outside, they've all got a nervous tremor of some kind, sweetheart. The world is a big hospital, and I am a nurse in it, George. The whole world's a big hospital, a big neurological ward and I am a student nurse in it. I guess that's still my job![15]

Moving indeed is this timorous and faint hope that with gentle care the sick may be healed after all.

Jean-Paul Sartre's novel *Nausea*[16] is a work that will probably last a long time as a relentless commentary on the tormented mind of modern man. The title is intended, I suppose, as an imaginative summary of human life in the twentieth century. Roquentin, the hero of *Nausea*, is sickened by an acute awareness of the realities around him (the purple suspenders of the bartender, the chocolate-colored wall of the cafe), is sickened by his intellectual encounter with existence and the stickiness, the "sweetish" taste, the "gelatinous slither" of the "naked World." The transitory portion of Sartre's metaphor is the literal nausea ("I wanted to vomit"), the revolt of the stomach. The enduring portion of the metaphor is the metaphysical anguish by which modern man is oppressed through the discovery of his freedom and the anxiety aroused by the dawning awareness of his being in a world where there are no signs to tell him who he is or where to go or what to do.

In the famous scene in the park where Roquentin in a mystical adventure finds the key to Existence, Roquentin says, "I would so like to let myself go, forget myself, sleep. But I can't. I'm suffocating: existence penetrates me everywhere, through the eyes, the nose, the mouth. . . . The Nausea has not left me and I don't believe it will leave me soon; but I no longer have to bear it, it is no longer an illness or a passing fit: it is I."

At the expense of (and oversimplifying, of course) Sartre's extraordinarily penetrating insights, one might venture the emendation: I am sick, therefore I exist; or—I exist, ergo I am sick! There is something of this, though, in existential philosophy—per-

---

[15]Tennessee Williams, *Period of Adjustment* (New York, 1960), Act III.
[16]Sartre (Norfolk, Connecticut, 1959). *La Nausee* was first published in 1938 by Librairie Gallimard.

haps that is why it seems to say so much about modern man and his predicament. Roquentin's "fascination" with the root of the chestnut tree explains his nausea, the nausea that follows the invasion of existence, that attends the slow awareness of being, of being that is simply *there,* outside "the world of explanations and reasons" and that weighs "heavily on your heart like a great motionless beast."

But with Sartre, as I observed earlier, there is a cure for this illness. The sickness is not quite unto death. Sartre's philosophy of health lies in the leap or act of commitment. Sickness and suffering come of aimlessness, and existence is aimless except as man gives it aim and purpose. To be well, then, is to be committed, to be bound, if only within, as Wordsworth said, the scanty limits of the sonnet. Whether the cure is effective or not, or whatever we may think of the cure or the sickness as Sartre presents it, modern man, in a great deal of modern literature, is, figuratively and literally, one way or another, unmistakably ill.[17]

A Local Habitation and a Name

In this essay I have selected for discussion those metaphors in the literature of our time which I think are the most revealing. There are others, of course, which deserve attention, more serious attention, perhaps, if we had the benefit of hindsight, than those I have chosen to write about. However, let it suffice for the time being to examine briefly as follows a few of those I have neglected.

When Gertrude Stein used the term "lost" to characterize the younger generation of the 1920s, she hit, apparently, upon an apt and descriptive metaphor; but it has somewhat more of substance to it than a mere tag. For the "lost" in 1925 becomes the "stranger" in 1945, the stranger lost in a world where there are no signs, the man, as someone has said in reference to Camus' novel *The Stranger,* "who is lived by life." And in 1955, the

---

[17]It is revealing that Thomas Mann should have chosen a sanitarium as the setting for his best known novel, *The Magic Mountain,* one of the great works of our time. It is significant also that widespread sickness is the framework for an important contemporary European novel, *The Plague* by Albert Camus.

lost generation is the "beat generation," which in its seeming indifference and passivity (allowing itself, as it were, to be lived by life) raises up its voice not in praise and not in anger but in a howl. The title which Allan Ginsberg chose for his by now well-known poem, *Howl*, is in itself a striking modern metaphor, destined, I suspect, for a long life as the beat generation's description of the modern malaise.[18]

A widely used metaphor of our time originates, I think, in Dostoevsky's *Notes from Underground* where the main character is the "underground" man, one who has hidden himself away from the world, in this case determined to live and think as he pleases though his thoughts and his behavior may be contemptible in his as well as in other's eyes. "Underground" has been used as a figure of speech for some time in connection with the world of crime and in times of political revolution. It came vigorously back into circulation, of course, during the occupation of France in World War II and has remained to suggest a variety of emotions, largely, I think, resistance to an enemy, whoever the enemy may be.

The metaphor of life as a game of chance has been a favorite similitude for a long time, most telling probably in the late nineteenth century, and deriving possibly from the theory of evolution from which it was inferred that a good deal that happens in life depends upon chance. Thomas Hardy's poem "Hap" is readily remembered for its image of the dice. But despite widespread playing of games of chance today, the metaphor appears not to have the vitality it once had.

The metaphor, if it is a metaphor, of the "encounter," especially the "divine encounter," as used by existentialist philosophers and theologians may well be one of the most significant of our time. I suspect that the poetry of William Butler Yeats, if studied with a view to selecting its most compelling metaphors, would yield rich meaning, perhaps the richest and most valuable meaning of our time, in terms of the dream, the vision, and the message. Simone Weil's divine encounter as she describes it in

---

[18]Of the steel sculpture *Iron Throat* by Theodore Roszak, Peter Selz says; "This canine-human head is the portrait bust of a scream—agony, terror, warning." (*New Images of Man, op. cit.*)

Waiting for God may be closely related to the dedicated attention Yeats gives to the "vision."

In isolating these metaphors and examining them for what they tell us about ourselves and our world, there emerges a not very pleasant picture of modern life. I should like to conclude this essay with scenes of happier vistas and lovelier landscapes. In terms of the way we *talk* about ourselves and our world, the landscapes of our imagination are not lovely; instead, to borrow a phrase from Henry James, ours is the "imagination of disaster." Yet something has been accomplished in this essay which offers hope. We see that the *way* we choose to talk about experience tells us more about ourselves, about our beliefs, feelings, hopes, fears, intentions than about the true nature of the world itself. And the way we feel about ourselves is, as a matter of fact, of very considerable importance. There are still the *possibilities*— and the possibilities depend (that is, their coming to pass depends) on how we talk about *them*.

The sixteenth century saw the possibility of witches, daemons, ghosts, and Satan himself. The Elizabethans saw the possibility of blithe spirits, cherubim, seraphim, and archangels. The seventeenth century loved gardens. The eighteenth century saw nature methodized, but was urban and saw prisons and graves too. The nineteenth liked nature, and some few poets begged a return to the simplicity of country life and to the joy and healing powers of nature, but they did so in part because the rest of the nineteenth century saw all too clearly the possibility of machines and the world as a vast factory; and the twentieth century sees the possibility of the whole world as a hospital.

Purposely, of course, I am over-simplifying. Yet if we may judge from the enduring literature of the seventeenth century, that age of persecution and bloody civil wars could and did see the possibility of the world as a garden. The poets rejoiced without effort—in scores of splendid verses—in the plenitude and loveliness of all creation, in heaven's beauties and in earth's bounties, in fragrant blossoms, fair flowers, fruitful trees, sweet herbs, in the violet and the damask rose, in daffodils, the yew and holly, in meadows, vales, mountains, fields and fountains, in

77

abundant oceans and far off fertile lands and teeming forest. If Adam and Eve were expelled from Eden, might they not some day be allowed to return? There is that supremely beautiful speech of the Duke of Burgundy in Shakespeare's *King Henry V* when, pleading with the Kings of France and England, he asks what impediment there is that

> the naked, poor and mangled Peace,
> Dear nurse of arts, plenties and joyful births,
> Should not in this best garden of the world,
> Our fertile France, put up her lovely visage.

There is the possibility of peace and of fertile lands. Indeed, the seventeenth-century poets were so fond of the garden of the world, their saddest thoughts were those that spoke of leaving it, which spoke of mutability, of decay and death. For Andrew Marvell, earth's gardens are lovely beyond compare, and when he thinks of fleeting time and of death his image is of a desert—

> But at my back I alwaies hear
> Times winged Charriot hurrying near:
> And younder all before us lye
> Desarts of vast Eternity.

There may be very good reasons why modern man is preoccupied with images of sickness, of prisons, of monsters, why, in literature at least, he often "howls" in anguish like a "sick" machine performing "prison-like" tasks in a "wasteland," but there have been ages and times when he saw the possibility of being something quite different—"human," if nothing more, the measure of all things, frail but reasonable, and possibly heroic. And there have been times when philosopher and artist together saw the possibility of some "far-off divine event," some vision, in which they had unshakable faith.

The insights of the great writer are expressed with an accuracy so precise, so faithful to the facts, that if we would know the temper of an age, we turn to him. He brings the transitory images and the enduring ideas together in unerring imaginative syntheses. But when the predominant metaphorical expressions of an age are gathered together, it is seen that though the transitory parts, the extensional objects, are many and varied, the enduring parts, the intensional ideas, are almost invariably the same. By the device of pointing to the right object, to the one that is vivid and meaningful—to prisons, hospitals, machines, boats, gambling tables, gardens, deserts, insects, pilgrims, garbage cans, bridges, candles, lions, domes of many colored glass, whirlpools—the writer gives a local habitation and a name to those airy nothings, to faith, freedom, health, knowledge, beauty, peace—stubborn intuitions—which he will not let go of and which will not let go of him.

The Language of Criticism

B ᴇɪɴɢ ʟᴇᴀʀɴᴇᴅ in any branch of knowledge consists in being able to make statements of fact about a subject. This is the mood in which for the most part our organization and communication of knowledge is cast. Open any book of exposition on any subject, any history or manual or textbook, and you will find that the language, like the sentence I am now writing, is almost exclusively in the indicative mood; that is, it is in the mood of the statement of fact or truth. For instance, at random I open to this:

> During the Middle Ages painting, serving somewhat as the handmaiden of the Church, concentrated on embellishing the thoughts and doctrines of Christianity. Toward the end of this period, the painters, along with other thinkers in Europe, began to be interested in the natural world. Inspired by the new emphasis on man and the universe about him the Renaissance artist dared to confront nature, to study her deeply and searchingly, and to depict her realistically.[1]

Presumably, this is a statement of fact about painting and the evolution of painting in Europe. However, since we know that every utterance, because it is declarative, is not necessarily "right" or "fact" or "law," we tend to take these statements as standard observations subject to review and possible revision. They are at least a good place from which to start in the study of Renaissance art. The language in which the idea is presented says that the idea is a verifiable fact; but we make the mental reservation that the statement is what the author presently believes to be a just and supportable one about Western art.

Nevertheless, the indicative mood presents thoughts as though they were the substantial and irrefragable truth. "The writing in this novel is very beautiful" is a sentence one might find in a critical review; and what the sentence says is that the writing *is* beautiful, though the critic probably knows well enough that this is *his* feeling about it, that this is the way the

---

[1] Morris Kline, *Mathematics in Western Culture* (New York, 1953), p. 126.

prose style appeals to him. However, if a critic says, "Richard Wagner is inferior to Meyerbeer," we may agree or disagree, but the sentence says—as presumably the critic believes, and, therefore, intended the sentence to say—that Wagner *is* inferior to Meyerbeer, in the same sense that "strychnine is poisonous." If we do not know the music of Wagner or Meyerbeer or that they were composers and wrote operas, and if someone we trust—our teacher, for example—tells us that the one is inferior to the other, then the statement is not a judgment or an opinion but as surely a statement of fact as "Meyerbeer was twenty-two years older than Richard Wagner."[2] The language of criticism, or rather of a certain kind of criticism, is vigorously dogmatic, and whereas we trust the indicative when it is used in scientific writing, we must invariably see or hear works of art for ourselves if we are to evaluate statements made about them in critical writing. Unless we are on guard, we may allow sentences that are expressions of ardently biased feeling to appeal to us as though they were the pronouncements of massive authority.

It has been said that the critic should formulate his opinions with precision, as though what makes an opinion true or false depends upon the way it is uttered. On the contrary, what makes an opinion *believed* depends upon the way it is uttered, and where, and when. As an undergraduate I was given to understand in no uncertain terms that Tennyson was a third-rate poet with all the provincialism of a typical Victorian and that "Locksley Hall" is a silly adolescent exercise. Though presented as fact, critical statements are often statements of personal taste supported by whatever literary school is fashionable at the moment.

Let us examine a somewhat more complicated observation from the literature of criticism. In an essay on "Sir Christopher Wren," Aldous Huxley says:

> The Renaissance, as it spread, like some marvelous infectious disease of the spirit, across the face of Europe, manifested itself

---

[2]There is not a single opinion in literature which one cannot easily fight with its precise opposite." Anatole France, "The Disputes of the Flute Players," in *A Modern Book of Criticism*, ed. Ludwig Lewisohn (New York, 1919), p. 14.

in different countries by different symptoms. In Italy, the country of its origin, the Renaissance was, more than anything, an outburst of painting, architecture, and sculpture. Scholarship and religious reformation were, in Germany, the typical manifestations of the disease. But when this gorgeous spiritual measles crossed the English Channel, its symptoms were almost exclusively literary. The first premonitory touch of the infection from Italy "brought out" Chaucer. With the next bout of the disease England produced the Elizabethans. But among all these poets there was not a single plastic artist whose name we so much as remember.[3]

It is, we may agree, acceptable to say that the Renaissance manifested itself in different countries in different ways. But to say that the Renaissance was a "disease" confuses matters. We know that Huxley means that the Renaissance *spread* over Europe as an infectious disease spreads. But the metaphor is ill-chosen. As the figure is developed, it becomes a statement of fact: "Scholarship and religious reformation were, in Germany, the typical manifestations of the disease."

If we take Huxley at his word, scholarship and religious reformation were, then, symptoms of a sickness; and one way or another English literature of the Elizabethan age was the result of a "gorgeous spiritual measles." If Huxley's comment says anything at all, what it says is that the Renaissance was a disease. And anyone who would say that, to use a remark of George Bernard Shaw's, would say anything. It is neither true nor false nor communicative. It is at best misleading; that is, the language is misleading. Even the lay reader might well wonder what this Renaissance could have been, a disease which "brought out" Chaucer, and in a bout of it, like the plague, produced the Elizabethans. That the infection "brought out" Chaucer suggests that he fled his plague-stricken house, or broke out in blotches; and "gorgeous" spiritual measles could mean "resplendently beautiful" or "elegant" spiritual measles, which does not make sense.

It is necessary to exercise eternal vigilance over our language if for no other reason than that a reader tends to believe the writer because what is said is said in the way it is said; that is, as fact.

---

[3] Aldous Huxley, "Sir Christopher Wren," in *On Art and Artists* by Aldous Huxley, ed. Morris Philipson (New York, 1960). "Sir Christopher Wren" was first published in *On the Margin* in 1923.

Consider another illustration of the language of criticism, a memorable passage from *Mont-Saint-Michel and Chartres* by Henry Adams. The following occurs in the last pages of Chapter X, "The Court of the Queen of Heaven." Adams is talking about the stained-glass windows above the high altar.

> The sermon of Chartres, from beginning to end, teaches and preaches and insists and reiterates and hammers into our torpid minds the moral that the art of the Virgin was not that of her artists but her own. . . .
>
> Therefore, when we, and the crushed crowd of kneeling worshippers around us, lift our eyes at last after the miracle of the mass, we see, far above the high altar, high over all the agitation of prayer, the passion of politics, the anguish of suffering, the terrors of sin, only the figure of the Virgin in majesty, looking down on her people, crowned, throned, glorified, with the infant Christ on her knees. . . . She does not assert herself; probably she intends to be felt rather than feared. . . . She is not exaggerated either in scale, drawing, or colour. She shows not a trace of self-consciousness, not an effort for brilliancy, not a trace of stage effect—hardly even a thought for herself, except that she is at home, among her own people. . . . [The ability of the artist] is never in doubt, and if he has kept true to the spirit of the western portal and the twelfth century, it is because the Virgin of Chartres was the Virgin of Grace, and ordered him to paint her so. . . .
>
> For seven hundred years Chartres has seen pilgrims, coming and going more or less like us, and will perhaps see them for another seven hundred years; but we shall see it no more, and can safely leave the Virgin in her majesty, with her three great prophets on either hand, as calm and confident in their own strength and in God's providence as they were when Saint Louis was born, but looking down from a deserted heaven, into an empty church, on a dead faith.[4]

The language here has a special quality. There is something intrinsic to the style that says the writer has credentials. We are disarmed and ready to listen. In Adams' writing there is a perceptiveness, a talent, which is something in addition to what he *knows* about Chartres. He *does* something, at it were, with his material.

To be sure, the dogmatic mood of the indicative is present, but it is used to support the ideas rather than to serve as a vehicle for pronouncements. Though syntactically declarative, the

---

[4]Henry Adams, *Mont-Saint-Michel and Chartres* (Boston, 1933), pp. 192 ff. Adams' idea here is presented in full stature in the chapter "The Dynamo and the Virgin" in his *The Education of Henry Adams*.

statements are statements of personal interpretation. The Virgin "does not assert herself; probably she intends to be felt rather than feared. . . . She shows not a sign of self-consciousness, not an effort for brilliancy, not a trace of stage effect." Statements that might, in other verbal surroundings, be crude declarations of truth or fact are here subtly modulated to take on a new character and virtue. That is, the statements of fact become statements of belief. They are columns that hold up the edifice of the idea.

After we have mastered the idea, we may disagree with it—even disapprove of it. In Adams' last quoted paragraph, an idea is created out of the materials of subject, style, and belief. The idea is not an opinion, nor is it fact. It is original and is expressed in what we might call the "creative" mood. It is not only about something, it *is* something. True, one takes it or leaves it. If one takes it, his life—or at least his frame of mind, his attitudes—may well be altered as a result; if one leaves it, one goes about one's business untouched.

Vocabulary

It might be said that the study of any subject consists in learning the vocabulary of the subject; and the wider the knowledge of the vocabulary, the more sophisticated the knowledge of the subject. If we know what a word means, really means, in all its complex references, we know the organization of the knowledge of which it is a part. If I know the meaning of the word "logarithm," I know the mathematics to which it refers; that is, I know how to use it in a mathematical context so as to communicate with someone else who also knows what the word means. In criticism, however, the technical words are relatively few. There is an original language for mathematics which must be learned and used as given. This is not the case with talk about literature and the arts, or with communication among artists. All words are serviceable for criticism.

When Berlioz discusses Beethoven's *Sixth Symphony* (the "Pastoral"), this is the way he talks about the first movement:

This astonishing landscape seems as if it were the joint work of Poussin and Michelangelo. The composer of Fidelio and of the

84

Eroica wishes in this symphony to depict the tranquility of the country and the peaceful life of the shepherds. The herdsmen begin to appear in the fields, moving about with their usual nonchalant gait; their pipes are heard afar and near. Ravishing phrases caress one's ears deliciously, like perfumed breezes. Flocks of chattering birds fly overhead; and now and then the atmosphere seems laden with vapors; heavy clouds flit across the face of the sun, then suddenly disappear, and its rays flood the fields and woods with torrents of dazzling splendor. These are the images evoked in my mind by hearing this movement; and I fancy that, in spite of the vagueness of instrumental expression many hearers will receive the same impressions.[5]

Though written by a composer, this appreciation of the "Pastoral" is anything but technical; and Berlioz is universally admired, I believe, as a critic.

If a handbook (complete with glossary) for criticism of the arts were established at some congress of critics, there would then be a way of discussing a painting or a poem which could be common to all critics. We feel spontaneously that this would be a calamity for criticism—and for the arts. The very strength and catholicity of the arts come of their not being part of a rigorously defined body of knowledge. A work of art is, momentarily, a fragment of life apprehended at once and as it happens; and to parcel off literature, for instance, as a distinct area of learning, would be to abstract it from life—from the singular, that is—which would destroy it. The same may be said for criticism, which deals also with the unique fragment of life and is also an art.

So if one is to talk about the arts, he talks about all life experiences, and all words are fitting and suitable. A work of literature *can* be discussed sociologically, biologically, economically, psychoanalytically, anthropologically in the vocabulary of those disciplines—in terms, for instance, of "milieu," "evolution," "the unconscious," "ritual," "dialectical materialism." And the insights derived from application of, say, a theory of society to a work of literature may be valuable and enriching; but one can never say all there is to be said about a work of art either sociologically or psychoanalytically or through any single systematic method of analysis.

---

[5] Quoted in *Orchestral Music: An Armchair Guide* by Lawrence Gilman, ed. Edward Cushing, New York, 1951, p. 45.

Writers of criticism have sometimes formulated their own technical vocabularies; but as a rule their terminology remains unique and personal. When other critics use the term "objective correlative," acknowledgment is usually made to T. S. Eliot, to whom the phrase belongs. Credit is still given to William Empson for his "ambiguity," and to Kenneth Burke for his "symbolic action." Because these terms mean only what their authors intend they shall mean, because the arts and criticism are highly individualistic activities—creations of single identifiable talents— eccentric terminologies do not enter the public domain for a long time. Even today when we speak of "catharsis" in the definition of tragedy, we think of Aristotle and probably name him.

Though not a terminology, there is in the language of modern criticism a way of speaking, a new idiom that, when used by R. P. Blackmur or Kenneth Burke, can be the vehicle of apercus scarcely to be intimated without it. This new idiom enlarges meaning by the use of two devices. First, there is the use of etymology. In R. P. Blackmur's essay (entitled "Unappeasable and Peregrine") on T. S. Eliot's *Four Quartets,* Blackmur quotes the line "Old men ought to be explorers" (from "East Coker") and interprets it with assistance from the etymology of the word "explore," which, he notes, has the root meaning, "to cry out." "The mind should cry out upon what it finds, for that is the burden of the word 'explore' . . . and that is the burden of this poem."[6]

Second, there is the novel device of applying words ordinarily used in one context to illuminate another context, refreshing the words with new and multiple meaning. Kenneth Burke is one of the most stimulating of modern critics. The opulence of his intellectual equipment is attested to by the multitude and density of the ideas which range upon his pages. Taking words out of their conventional contexts, he speaks of works of art as strategies for dealing with situations, of poems as prayers, of social beliefs as pious or impious.

By virtue of his interdisciplinary lexicon, Burke offers a way

---

[6] R. P. Blackmur, *Form & Value in Modern Poetry* (New York, 1952), p. 154.

of talking about poetry that affords new insights into creative activity:

> To be sure, when we attempt to extend our pseudo-statements into the full complexity of life, we meet with considerable *recalcitrance*. But so does the poet meet with considerable recalcitrance in arranging the materials of his poem. We must "altruistically" take into account the order of difficulty that goes with the order of our intentions. The factor of recalcitrance may force us to alter our original strategy of expression greatly. And in the end, our pseudo-statements may have been so altered by the revisions which the recalcitrance of the material has forced upon us that we can now more properly refer to them as *statements*. . . . A statement is a completed pseudo-statement — which is to say that *a statement is an attitude rephrased in accordance with the strategy of revision made necessary by the recalcitrance of the materials employed for embodying this attitude.*[7]

R. P. Blackmur has amplified meaning through an augmented and rejuvenated critical language. In an essay on "W. B. Yeats: Between Myth and Philosophy," Blackmur says:

> Aubrey Beardsley once told Yeats—and Yeats liked to repeat it—that he put a blot of ink on paper and shoved it around till something came. This is one routine hair-raising practice of the artist of any sort: to invoke that which *had been* unknown, to insist on the apparition, to transform the possible into a vision. The artist poaches most on his resources when ad libbing, when he meets, and multiplies, his perils with, as Yeats said nonchalance.[8]

In other words, the poet *ad libs* around the idea of the poem, around the protogenic materials, drawing as he is able on his resources until the "perils" (compare Burke's "pseudo-statements") have been met and arranged through "progressive interaction," where opposites are used not for contradiction but for development into an ambiguity "deeper than the particular words of the poem."

True, this way of talking about a literary work seems sometimes to be a worrying of words, a stalking of the prey with intent to force its secret life into the open; and sometimes it is only a straining at gnats. Then, too, this kind of criticism offers the golden opportunity for making gnomic utterances that on the surface seem of ultimate profundity but which, when sub-

---

[7]Kenneth Burke, *Permanence and Change* (New York, 1935), p. 327.
[8]R. P. Blackmur, *op. cit.*, p. 154.

87

jected to careful examination, turn out to be perilously close to nonsense.

The Aesthetic Adjective

Some years ago in his *Practical Criticism*, I. A. Richards called attention to the semantic phenomenon of the aesthetic adjective. He observed that the adjectives used in talking about a work of art often tell more about the user than about that to which they refer. When we call something "beautiful" or "ugly," we are talking about our feeling toward it, not about the thing itself. The aesthetic adjective is a staple ingredient in criticism, and we could scarcely do without it; but now and again it is over-used, now and again it is used in the mistaken belief that something of grave importance is being said.

The most learned of critics are, on occasion, carried away by the sound of adjectives seriatim, as in this from Eric Bentley in *The Playwright as Thinker*. Speaking of T. S. Eliot's play, *The Family Reunion,* Bentley says: "Its success and failure are exactly opposite to those of [Eugene O'Neill's] *Mourning Becomes Electra.* Eliot's 'conception' is clear, noble, and mature, his 'communication' uncertain, irregular, and incomplete. O'Neill's 'communication' is rapid, strong, almost overwhelming, his 'conception' is rude, simple-minded, gaga."[9] Bentley's comment on O'Neill's dramatic sensibility tells us little about *Mourning Becomes Electra* but a great deal about Bentley's own tastes and dramatic sensibility.

In *The Quintessence of Ibsenism*, George Bernard Shaw cites an article in "The Daily Telegraph for the 14th March 1891" which compares Ibsen's *Ghosts* "to an open drain, a loathsome sore unbandaged, a dirty act done publicly, or a lazar house with all its doors and windows open." The epithets used in the article (presumably *describing* Ibsen's play) include: "bestial, cynical, disgusting, poisonous, sickly, delirious, indecent, loathsome, fetid, literary carrion, crapulous stuff, clinical confessions." The message is reasonably clear: The author of the article disliked and intensely disapproved of *Ghosts.*

---

[9]Eric Bentley, *The Playwright as Thinker* (New York, 1955), p. 187.

In journalistic criticism the aesthetic adjective is used to excess. The professional critic appears to have always a large and varied stock of applicable words ready for any occasion. If a drama critic were writing a review of, say, a restoration comedy, he would be perfectly safe if he larded his column with such words as foppish, affected, satirical, high-spirited, ribald, gay, bawdy, witty, dashing, mannered, droll, irreverent, gallant. There is little value to this coin; more and more words are needed in order to buy even a small idea. Indeed, many daily reviews of motion pictures, concerts, plays, exhibitions present few if any developed ideas, and in the instance of motion pictures, as with restaurants and motels, stars can be used to indicate degrees of distinction.

IMPRESSIONISM

Though "impressionistic" criticism is today generally condescended to as amusing, now and then revealing, but scarcely, for scholarship or letters, valuable or significant, the language of "impressionism" is of interest to us here. By and large the purpose of impressionistic criticism is appreciation. In the hands of able critics like James Huneker and Paul Rosenfeld, there is much to be said for impressionism, which inspires the reader with the desire to see or read or hear for himself the work being discussed. It is of historical interest that this kind of criticism should have flourished around the turn of the century, related as it was to impressionism in painting and music and to symbolism in drama, poetry, and design. At the moment, however, we shall examine only its language. Here is a passage from Paul Rosenfeld's "Debussy," in his book *Musical Portraits*. Rosenfeld says of Debussy:

> He has permeated music completely with his impressionistic sensibility. His style is an image of this our pointillistically feeling era. With him impressionism achieves a perfect musical form. Structurally, the music of Debussy is a fabric of exquisite and poignant moments, each full and complete in itself. The harmonies are not, as in other compositions, preparations. They are apparently an end in themselves, flow in space, and then change hue, as a shimmering stuff changes. For all its golden earthiness, the style of Debussy is the most liquid and impalpable of musical styles. It is forever gliding, gleaming, melting. . . . It is well-nigh edgeless. It

seems to flow through our perceptions as water flows through fingers. . . . His orchestration invariably produces all that is cloudy and diaphanous in each instrument. He makes music with flakes of light, with bright motes of pigment. His palette glows with the sweet, limpid tints of a Monet or a Pissarro or a Renoir. His orchestra sparkles with iridescent fires, with divided tones, with delicate violets and argents and shades of rose. The sound of the piano, usually but the ringing of flat colored stones, at his touch becomes fluid, velvety and dense, takes on the properties of satins and liqueurs. The pedal washes new tint after new tint over the keyboard.[10]

In Rosenfeld's criticism, the music is talked about as music, but also as something else. The harmonies "flow in space, and then change hue, as a shimmering stuff changes." We think of music as progressing in time; it is sound, not color; and it is not material, as a shimmering stuff is. But it is *like* something that flows in space; it irresistibly suggests color; it is like satin. Through some analogical mechanism of the mind the music seems to gleam, to melt; and we are able to possess the music a little, to know it, if we can find analogies that fall naturally into place.

Impressionistic criticism draws upon the vocabulary of the senses and talks about one sensation in terms of another. The sound of music is like the touch of water flowing through fingers; it suggests breezes, the feel of velvet and satin. It is like the fragrance of perfumes, the taste, texture, and color of liqueurs. In this kind of criticism one art is described in terms of another. The music is made with flakes of light, with pigment. Debussy's "palette" glows with limpid tints. His orchestration is diaphanous, with delicate violets and argents and shades of rose; and the pedal washes new tints over the keyboard.

Impressionistic criticism is not quite "creative" criticism; it is not expository; nor is it informative as practical knowledge. The writing has been inspired by the music, as music may be inspired by painting (Rachmaninoff's "Isle of the Dead"); as music may be inspired by a poem (Debussy's "Afternoon of a Faun"); and a dance inspired by music. Moreau's "Salome" drew a peroration from Huysmans, and Oscar Wilde's *Salome* inspired some of Aubrey Beardsley's finest drawings.

---

[10]Paul Rosenfeld, *Musical Portraits* (New York, 1920), pp. 121 ff.

It used to be said that the writings in Whitman's *Leaves of Grass* are not poems because the lines do not scan according to traditional methods of metrical measurement in English verse. That is, to become a poem, words must be arranged so that they make a pattern of accented and unaccented syllables. If the words do not make a pattern, they do not constitute a poem, because all poems, to be poems, must be capable of metrical measurement. However, because the writings in *Leaves of Grass* have other features in common with other wholly acceptable "poems," and perhaps because standard arrangement of accented and unaccented syllables is no longer considered a major and important feature of poetry, we are at liberty to call "Out of the Cradle Endlessly Rocking" a poem.

Much printer's ink has been spilled in critical wars, and many of these wars have been fought over whether certain pieces of literature and art are really literature or really art when it appears that they do not contain those elements which are common to (or have always been common to) literature and art, which is to say that they do not fit into accepted definitions. One of the most prolonged of these quarrels revolves around the argument that there can be no true tragedy in the theatre of the twentieth century because tragedy, by definition, is impossible in a mass culture where there are no heroes of noble stature to fall from a high place. The arguments pro and con are well known and scarcely need to be reviewed here.

Aristotle's *Poetics* is one of the most celebrated of all critical works. We remember, however, that Aristotle prepared his rules for tragedy after having arrayed before him the great dramas of his time for the purpose of finding those features common to them all. The profound emotional effect of these dramas being so universally experienced, their dramatic intensity and eloquence so universally admired, they served as the very best material with which a philosopher could work. Aristotle singled out the main common ingredients of Greek tragic drama, gave them names, and put them into a form of critical exposition which has been used ever since for purposes of prescription and evaluation. Newly interpreted, or used as a starting point, the

Poetics is an incomparable instrument of analysis. We should remember, however, that not even Aristotle said *all* there is to be said about drama, past or present.

It is a great temptation to agree with Anatole France when he says, "The good critic is he who relates the adventures of his soul among masterpieces." In general, modern criticism has heartily disagreed with this opinion. In Chapter I of *Theory of Literature,* Rene Wellek and Austin Warren have this to say about creative criticism.

> Some theorists would simply deny that literary study is knowledge and advise a "second creation," with results which to most of us seem futile today—Pater's description of Mona Lisa or the florid passages in Symonds or Symons. Such "creative criticism" has usually meant a needless duplication or, at most, the translation of one work of art into another, usually inferior.[11]

We remember also T. S. Eliot's aversion to criticism which is of the "creative order." In his essay on "Hamlet," Eliot warns against critics whose "minds often find in Hamlet a vicarious existence for their own artistic realization." In writing about *Hamlet,* Goethe and Coleridge should have remembered, he says, that the "first business" of the critic is "to study a work of art. . . . We should be thankful," Eliot continues, "that Pater did not fix his attention on this play."

One should not lightly take up a quarrel with T. S. Eliot. He is much too formidable a critic, and what he says in this passage is "right" for our time—though we cannot help observing that like everything else in the context of society, fashions in critical writing are now in, now out of style and favor.

The first business of a critic is "to study a work of art." But there are many ways of studying a work of art. Rainer Maria Rilke's essay on *Rodin* is an example, so I think, of incontestably superior criticism. Using one of Coleridge's definitions of criticism, *Rodin* elucidates "the beauties of an original work" in "a sustained dignity of language." We note at once that there is no

---

[11]Rene Wellek and Austin Warren, *Theory of Literature* (New York, 1949), p 3.

terminology in Rilke's language. We see also that the manner of expression is not dogmatic, because for one thing dogmatism is not called for. This criticism is not interested in opinion versus fact. Nor is it aggressive. The sculptures of Rodin are not attacked frontally; the criticism is not on target but radiates around the works discussed. Without our being aware of it, something is happening in connection with the sculptures that we are presently surprised and delighted to discover has happened. They have moved, as it were. Nor does Rilke intrude between reader and work of art as do some academic critics, who would have us believe that what they are saying about the work is more important than the work itself. Rilke's criticism springs from the belief that art is not a prescription for conduct (something to be talked about sermonically) but an end in itself. In many ways, Rilke's essay supports J. E. Spingarn's contention (in his "The New Criticism") that the creative and the critical instinct are one and the same, that "in their flashes of insight taste and genius are one."

There are many kinds of criticism, as we have already observed, and I do not know that one is so much better than another, depending upon what we ask of it. The creative certainly has its place for those moments when we ask for nothing except to admire.

Somewhere, James Huneker said about criticism, "Be as profound as you please, but be amusing." Elsewhere, in *Promenades of an Impressionist,* he says of critics:

> One thing is certain—a man writing in terms of literature about painting, an art in two dimensions, cannot interpret fully the meanings of the canvas, nor can he be sure that his opinion, such as it is, when it reaches the reader, will truthfully express either painter or critic. . . . Criticism is at two removes from its theme. Therefore criticism is makeshift. Therefore, let critics be modest and allow criticism to become an amiable art.[12]

In spite of Huneker, criticism is mostly an unamiable art. It is corrective; it finds fault. The connotation attached to the word "criticism" in its common usage is that it is a manner of speaking, pontifically and solemnly, in the negative.

---

[12]James Huneker, *Promenades of an Impressionist* (New York, 1910), p. 283.

Criticism ought always to be amiable, and amusing, and profound. The purpose of criticism is to teach, to serve as guide in the development of taste, in methods of analysis, in appreciation, and in knowledge. There are no boundaries to criticism; there is no prepared language or handbook. Criticism is the art of teaching at its highest level; and all the resources of language and all the resources of learning in the various intellectual and artistic endeavors are at the service of criticism, as they are of literature and art. To be a first-rate critic one has almost to take all knowledge for his province, and the wider the knowledge the richer the criticism and, incidentally, the deeper the humility. If we wish to encounter the wonders of the imaginative and intellectual worlds, we need a guide—someone who has been among many wonders before, who is not afraid of them, who is still in awe of them, and who knows the destination and the way to go.

The Rhetoric of the Absurd

WHEN THE LOGIC of the outer world of "facts" no longer corresponds harmoniously with the logic of the inner world of thought, we recognize the absurd. Disenchantment in this respect has a steady rhythm, and we become accustomed to it, that is, we learn to adjust to the difference between what *is* and what we think *should be.* There are times, however, when what happens is so severely inconsistent with what we think should happen that we stagger before the event and only by an effort do we learn to accept it.

Philosophically, we ought not to be astonished at what happens. The event *has* taken place. Therefore, philosophically, we can accommodate the outer to the inner with a system of the absurd. It might be said, in forming a philosophy of the absurd, that when we are properly disillusioned, we have rid ourselves of an untruth. When we despair at making the outer coincide with the inner, it is philosophically sound to show that they do *not* correspond, to show the absurdity. The modern revolution in thought is a revolt against the incongruous by elevating the incongruous to a position of truth.

We are constantly at work transmuting the incongruous in thought and experience into the congruous; nevertheless, a one-to-one correspondence between the inner and the outer is less easily imagined than the absurd, because, indeed, the absurd *is.* If we could imagine a pattern of immutable consistencies, we would have created a world. It is more in line with our present creative abilities, however, to imagine a bride and bridegroom flying through the air with the greatest of ease, as in a painting by Chagall.

In what follows, it is my intention to study the rhetoric of modern imaginative literature, the rhetoric which has developed out of the philosophy of the absurd, to examine the devices which the modern writer uses to present the absurdities, the incongruities, of our world.

Reversal is the major device of the rhetoric of the absurd. In literature and in art it is the deliberate substitution of the abnormal for the normal, of the unusual for the usual, of unreason for reason, of the unexpected for the expected, of the fantastic for the commonplace, of disorder for order, of the perverse for the prescriptive. Reversal asserts opposites with the weight of emphasis on the uncommon, the unexpected. Through the use of reversal a dramatic tension is created between the customary and the uncustomary, between the expected and the unexpected, with the accent on the unexpected as revelation of a new truth.

Consider, for example, the substitution of simultaneity for succession, which is a reversal of the traditional belief in cause and effect change in terms of an arrangement of several changes in a single vision, as in the paintings of the Cubists. We might note also the reversal that is found in the substitution of the non-logical for the logical in, for instance, the blending of traditional separate categories in the love-hate ambivalence delineated in modern literature. In the art and literature of the Dada movement, the incongruous is substituted for the congruous. According to Dada, the "ordinary" is no longer dependable, whereas the extraordinary is positive and reliable, discovered in a sudden freedom from the old logic. In Tristan Tzara's "Lecture on Dada" (1922), he says, "There is no logic. . . . The acts of life have no beginning or end. Everything happens in a completely idiotic way."

Temporarily, we are shocked by a reversal of the customary because mostly we are committed to the customary as the normal way of life. Often, however, the stronger the presentation of the abnormal, the stronger the belief in the normal.

Of Rimbaud, Camus says in *The Rebel,* "Life for him was 'a farce for the whole world to perform.' But on the day of his death, he cries out to his sister: 'I shall lie beneath the ground but you, you will walk in the sun!' "

The familiar is refreshed with new meaning when we return from the prodigalities of the imagination to the home of custom. When Gregor Samsa is transformed into an enormous insect, in

96

the story by Franz Kafka, not only is his contempt for himself aggravated by the reversal, but the plot's return to the normal at the end of the story is marked by a renewal of respect for the customary.

Reversal is also a method of philosophical inquiry into the measure of the difference between the normal and the abnormal, the human and inhuman, reason and unreason. The more horrible the Furies who pursue Orestes, the more human Orestes. This was the genius of Pallas Athena, that she knew the difference and inclined toward Orestes. The more inhuman a person behaves, the more admirable the human. The more we are accosted by unreason, the more we desire reason. The visions of madness offer new insights into the nature of reason itself and serve to elevate and recommend common sense.

A prevailing image in the literature of the absurd is the descent into unreason. This image is of great antiquity, and in western art we discover it first in Homer. In order that he may find his way home, that is, in order that he may return to the scenes and life of custom, Odysseus must first descend into Hades and there converse with the dead Tiresias who alone can direct him to Ithaca. This excursion into the dark unknown, it appears, is necessary if one would understand the value of the known. A glimpse into the abyss assures us of the rightness of solid ground. The descent is followed by a return to that old fondness for the world and its furnishings which we know with our human senses and our human intellect. The extremes of the older literature are used for the purpose of restoring to us that love for the world of the everyday, the normal, the "bliss of the commonplace," as Tonio Kroger puts it in the story by Thomas Mann.

The device of reversal is a favorite with modern writers and is used often with subtlety. But there is this difference between its use in the older literature and in the modern. Whereas in the history of western literature the descent into unreason and death is followed by an ascent into reason and life, in the modern literature of the absurd often only the descent is portrayed. In the old masters, order is restored, paradise is regained, Faust is redeemed, Fortinbras takes charge, and Alice returns from

Wonderland; in the modern, there is "no exit," the last hold on reality slips away, the caprice of the Castle reigns supreme, the normal is more false than the abnormal, non-being asserts itself in gibberish and the banal; rage prevails.

Even so, much of the literature of the absurd is esthetically satisfying. If the "normal" is identified with the "false," the opposite will have at least the virtue of "honesty."[1] Moreover, the absurd makes possible a catharsis of that rage and despair which some people feel toward the everyday world but are unable—or not permitted—to express.

Considered in the context of the novel, a striking example of reversal as a modern rhetorical device occurs in *Wise Blood* by the late Flannery O'Connor. Virtually the entire narrative and its meaning are developed through the use of reversal. Hazel Motes, the central figure of *Wise Blood*, a self-styled itinerant preacher, preaches in his singular way the "Church Without Christ," where one is redeemed not through belief but through disbelief, where there is no Jesus because there was no Fall and no Redemption. "The only way to truth is through blasphemy," he says. Later, following several extraordinary events, Hazel Motes has doubts about his new faith. One could not even believe in blasphemy as the way to salvation, "because then you were believing in something to blaspheme."

Hazel Motes has much to say on the subject of a Christian Church Without Christ. His talk is not only the opposite of what is expected, it is a determined reversal of belief. But Flannery O'Connor's purpose in *Wise Blood*, as I read the novel, is reinforcement of faith in Christ and His Church through this

---

[1]Reversal is, of course, a not uncommon technique in logic, and it is tempting to locate the first use of the modern rhetorical device of reversal in Hegel's dialectic of opposites where every negation is an affirmation. In the literature of the absurd, some writers defend negation as a movement toward a new affirmation, whereas the more tradition-oriented see negation as only a denial of that which has been affirmed.

The traditional device of rhetoric called "oxymoron" is used in the literature of the absurd to apply to categories as well as to single words. When we observe that something can be both what it is and not what it is, we have the absurd. Life is not as neat and tidy in the ordering of experience as it was once said in literature, philosophy, and history to be. In experience opposites often meet in unison and contraries are amalgamated. Reality is the full account.

device of reversal. As the narrative progresses, it becomes clear that Hazel Motes' determination not to believe is being undermined slowly but surely until finally he realizes the truth of the accepted faith and blinds himself that he may see it more clearly. The stronger his temptation to perversity, the stronger his faith in the given. This is not a new insight into the psychology of human conduct; what is especially provocative about *Wise Blood*, however, is Flannery O'Connor's use of the modern devices of reversal within reversal, image within contrary image, idea within contrary idea, paradox within paradox, the negation of the affirmed to the end that Hazel Motes' return to the faith must follow as the inescapable conclusion to a logical proposition.

In the literature of the absurd, only our inhumanity, it sometimes seems, is portrayed; but the purpose may well be the opposite—a good look at sickness may redefine health, a good look at villains may redefine heroes, escalations into narcotic trance may reassert the "bliss of the commonplace."

FANTASY

In his *A Brief Guide to the Exhibition of Fantastic Art, Dada, Surrealism*, Alfred H. Barr, Jr. says: "The explanation of the kind of art shown in this exhibition may be sought in the deep-seated and persistent interest which human beings have in the fantastic, the irrational, the spontaneous, the marvelous, the enigmatic, and the dreamlike." Barr goes on to say: "It is probable that at no time in the past four hundred years has the art of the marvelous and anti-rational been more conspicuous than at the present time."

Modern literature, too, makes use of the fantastic; but unlike its presentation in the graphic arts, where surrealism, for instance, may be readily observed as "marvelous, enigmatic, and dreamlike," the fantastic in the literature of the absurd is presented as not fantastic at all.[2] The wild imaginings of the absurd are not marvels, they are realities. The writer's use of fantasy

---

[2]Compare, for example, the surrealistic figures in the painting "Balcony I" by Kurt Seligmann with the characters in Genet's play, *The Balcony*.

is not an interest in the marvelous; it is a device used to shock the reader into acute awareness of the human condition in the twentieth century.

The marvelous and supernatural are very nearly always to be found in the epic poems of the past. "Tragedy should make men marvel, but the epic," says Aristotle in the *Poetics* "in which the audience does not witness the action, has greater scope for the inexplicable at which men marvel most." Often in the epic the marvelous is used to further the plot of the story, but at the same time, in the hands of a literary artist, it is metaphorical and has meaning as metaphor. That Circe can turn the gluttonous sailors of Odysseus into swine is a wonder, but that they behave *like* swine, or that Circe thinks of men as swine, is a metaphorical comment on human beings.

Fantasy as a rhetorical device in medieval story-telling was used to support and give strength to the ideals of the time. The miraculous happenings in *Sir Gawain and the Green Knight,* pointing as they do to the ideals of chivalry, courtesy, loyalty, Christian humility, were used by the author to give narrative substance to these ideals. In Chaucer the marvelous still adorns the moral and is full of wit and wisdom. The fantastic is often used in satire, as in the various voyages of Swift's Gulliver. The fantastic is used to entertain, presenting what might in another context be frightening or weird. One remembers Robert Burns' "Tam o' Shanter" and the hilarious ghostly doings around Alloway Kirk. Shakespeare, never at a loss for some ingenious magic to help the story along and aid in drawing conclusions about life, returned in *The Tempest* to an insubstantial pageant as the vehicle for the wisdom of his Prospero. Hawthorne, master of allegory, could spin a metaphor about the old nick himself into a critique of evil, of suspicion, and of faith.[3]

---

[3]It is interesting that children's stories have often depended for their fascination on magic and wondrous happenings. It seems that animals can often be made to utter truths about conduct and behavior better than friends, enemies, and parents. The art of Walt Disney is the classic modern example of the traditional fantasy, gay, entertaining, believable, with messages about good and evil interspersed among the doings. Contemporary Pop Art depends also on fantasy, and its basis seems to be satire through appeal to the irrational and incongruous. Contemporary advertising

In traditional rhetoric fantasy consisted in making the unnatural natural. In Homer, the Olympians are deities of supernatural powers; but they behave like human beings. In *Macbeth* the witches have extraordinary abilities, yet they, too, conduct their business as though they were human beings, albeit not very admirable ones. In *The Canterbury Tales,* a rooster and a hen are made to think and talk like a man and woman. In *Dracula* the vampires behave in a manner human.[4] Frankenstein's monster strives to become human, as do the robots in Capek's *R. U. R.*

In modern fantasy, however, the predicament is often reversed. In Ionesco's *Rhinoceros,* human beings become animals. In Kafka's *Metamorphosis,* a man becomes a huge insect. In Chaplin's *Modern Times,* a man behaves like a robot. Among the grotesque figures in the fiction of contemporary southern writers, some strive to be more like Frankenstein's monster and Bram Stoker's Dracula than "human beings." The modern literary artist gives a large measure of his attention to that which is unnatural and inhuman in human beings, offering the inhuman, ironically, as the human condition of which we are all, apparently, a part. Using the metaphor of reversal, he is saying that what defines our humanity is our inhumanity.

The Balcony by Jean Genet is an example of modern fantasy in the literature of the absurd. Here the characters appear to be "ordinary" human beings, that is to say, a bishop, a police chief, a judge, a general, prostitutes, photographers, revolutionaries. Their behavior, however, is fantastic, when measured by the daily lives of most people.

---

uses fantasy as a rhetorical device, and readers or listeners appear to accept this irrationalism without question, as though it were the most natural thing in the world for a dove to come flying sweetly through an open window, to say nothing of an electric iron, for a washing machine to grow ten feet tall, to say nothing of white knights who make spotless everything with a lance, and good witches who serve as hairdressers with instantaneous success.

[4] Of parenthetical interest, perhaps, what attracts our attention to those who live on the blood of others is not wholly the horror of the "fantastic" Count Dracula, a character in a novel, but the suggestion, through the use of the extended metaphor of the vampire, that there are some everyday human beings, half dead themselves, who live, figuratively speaking, on the blood of others.

The setting for *The Balcony* is an expensive and elegant house of prostitution that offers a variety of diverting entertainments all based on the principle of illusion. The several rooms of the house (Irma, who presides over them, says there are "thirty-eight studios! Every one of them gilded") are like stage-settings. The visitor chooses the "studio" suited to the role he wishes to play, and the establishment provides supporting characters, costumes, lighting, properties, even audiovisual aids. There is, for example, a funeral studio, a sacristy, a mausoleum. The judge plays the role of judge and is supported by an "executioner," who plays his role in pretending to whip the petty thief, one of Madame Irma's actresses, who in turn improvises her part to fit the moods of the judge.

The figures in *The Balcony* are not living persons; they are bloodless types playing the roles assigned to them by modern society. They are the *idea* of police chief, of judge, and so on; and they enact the parts expected of them in a manner amplified and magnified, so that we shall not mistake that for which they stand. They are fantastic in that they are embodied classifications rather than modulated human beings. In a world of illusion, to *be* is to be a certified abstraction of bishop, police chief, revolutionary. It is not what *they* say but what is said *about* them that matters. In his existential anxiety over non-being, the Chief of Police has his tomb prepared and descends into it to become (as he hopes) a fixed and monumental concept of glory, piety, justice, "larger than large, stronger than strong, deader than dead."

Personification[5]

In the Introduction to the Grove Press anthology, *Seven Plays of the Modern Theatre*, Harold Clurman says, "With purpose gone and action chiefly reflexive, little remains of character except contour. No wonder, then, that most of the figures in these plays are virtually anonymous." By contrast, the aim of

---

[5]Since all rhetorical devices are basically metaphor, any one will merge with another or others, making tidy classifications impossible. Personification, allegory, and fantasy, for example, are very often the same, serve, that is, the same purpose, of talking about one thing in terms of another.

nineteenth-century fiction and drama was the creation of warm-bodied, three dimensional characters, the presentation of that complex personality of a human being which identifies him as separate and unique and for this reason a moving force in the social setting. A whole gallery of such characters comes quickly to mind out of Thackeray, Dickens, George Eliot, Thomas Hardy, to mention only English novelists. With very considerable skill at their command, these authors created memorable, living people, each eccentric when compared with the others, each a force in the evolution of the social pattern. The characters do not stand for something, they are something. Moreover, though they are affected by their environment, they act upon it as much as they are acted upon by it.

In contemporary literature, character as an eccentric and determining force is not, it appears, as worthy of study as it was in the nineteenth century. Indeed, for modern tastes, character-drawing seems to be a homespun, quaint, antiquarian preoccupation. The figures in much of the literature of the absurd are personalities only in so far as they are affected by social forces or are at the mercy of compulsions, drives, fears of which they have little understanding and over which they have little control. In Camus' *The Stranger,* Meursault does not live life; he is lived by it. We say he is "the kind of person" who is alienated from a universe that is incomprehensible, that he is "anonymous" man. Meursault is brought into the foreground as a representative of the genus "anomie." He is anomie personified.

In the literature of the absurd, the figures often stand for metaphysical ideas or serve as illustrations of the effect on man of external social forces. They are often "type" characters and represent groups. Though the character of Antoine Roquentin in Sartre's *Nausea* is, as we say, "well-drawn," still what interests us perhaps more than his person is what he stands for. He is the carrier of existentialist ideas. *Nausea* is a novel in which existentialist philosophy is endowed with personality in the character of Roquentin. He is the personification of that mid-century sensibility that feels only disgust and a sick fury at the soilure of the world and the "stickiness" of existence. His physical nausea is the personification of his metaphysical distress.

In *Waiting for Godot,* the *dramatis personae* are not in a sense persons at all, though there is considerable difference between reading the play and seeing it in production where fine actors can turn the characters into living beings. Estragon and Vladimir are personifications of *everyman* in what is a modern morality play, of everyman who is waiting in varying degrees of patience for some sign, some message of good-will to come through the banality or terror of existence. *Waiting for Godot* is the dramatization of the modern predicament, superbly rendered by a dazzling craftsman of the theatre.

Though in *The Castle* and in *The Trial,* Franz Kafka created some memorable characters, especially the protagonist K., these novels are philosophical works and we read them as such. They are also modern tragedy in powerful form.

It has been said of Milton's fallen angels that in the initial debate in Hell each gives so rational and so eloquent an argument the attentive listener will be swayed first one way and then another. So it is with the characters in Kafka's novels, especially with the protagonist K. In *The Castle* each figure presents his case with such lucidity, with so impeccable a logic, with such infallible insight into his own predicament the reader cannot help being swayed first this way and then that. "How it is in reality we don't know," says the landlady, thinking of the whimsical ways of the Castle. But throughout the novel there is never any doubt about the beauty and rightness of K.'s reasoning. As a defendant at the bar, K. is the personification of rational man.

On the other hand, Klamm and the officials are guilty of unrelieved unreason, manifested by mystery, caprice, and inscrutable legalistic machinery. As inmates of the Castle, they represent the world of unreason. They are not called upon to explain themselves, for, frankly, as far as we can see, they are governed by an inexplicable bureaucratic instinct which appeals to human reason, that is to K., as capricious and wilful and inhuman. Klamm's behavior is beyond rational explanation, but what K. says about Klamm is, from the point of view of the mind of empirical man, absolutely and irrevocably right. Kafka's novels are interior monologues. To life's indictments his heroes reply dramatically and with exquisite logic, saying what any sane man, confronted with similar circumstances, would wish to say in his own defense.

Franz Kafka's K. is the personification of "reason" as most of us understand it, that is, eighteenth-century reason with its emphasis on law and order, with its dependence on a predictable regularity in events both human and non-human, relying on the certainty of cause and effect and on the virtues of systematic logic. The irony in Kafka's novels lies in this, that it is because his heroes subscribe to reason, because they are adroit in their use of it, that they are tragic figures, frustrated in everything they attempt to bring to pass. In the twentieth century, reason, personified by K., will not, it seems, justify the ways of man either to God or to his fellow men. Clear, limpid reason ought still to be capable of achieving the goal of understanding; but the unhappy truth is that it does not. Knowing this, Kafka and his heroes are stricken with an immedicable despair. The death of "Reason" is a tragedy of our time.

DICTION

Contemporary literature is notable for the freedom of its diction. A number of famous English words long imprisoned for linguistic assault and battery have been released, if not to enter polite letters at least to do certain literary jobs for which they seem peculiarly well-suited. Use of coarse and obscene language has become a kind of rhetorical strategy for shocking the reader into awareness of the contemporary setting; and in many instances (quite unrelated to pornography) foul language is called upon to express the emotions of rage, rebellion, disillusionment, suffering, and despair. Because such language has been in exile from literature for so long a time, it returns with a rare lustiness to intensify the rendition of these modern feelings. From the point of view of literary art, there is a danger in the use of obscene diction. It tends to be overused and becomes as banal and unimaginative as the weariest cliche. The use of such language has become almost an obsession with some writers, as though they could not utter the bad words often enough to make up for all the lost time when they were not permitted to use them.

Repetition has a certain power, but it is inflationary and depreciates in value as it is exaggerated.

The new freedom in writing and talking about sexual experience may also be discussed in terms of the rhetoric of the absurd. Some absurdist literature, at any rate, explores in various imaginative ways what might be called the sexual way of life, a genital orientation toward experience.[6] The prurient language of some modern works of fiction is often inventive and certainly vivid, sometimes oblique and suggestive, sometimes surrealistically libidinous; but mostly descriptions of sexual conduct derive their power from verbal simplicity and directness. The rhetoric of much modern erotic literature is notably lacking in the attenuations and refinements of literary art. It is intended that the words shall hit hard in direct frontal attack upon the reader's sensibilities and then retreat quickly before the arrival of the next paragraph. The diction used in the language of sex is often drawn from the vocabulary of narcotics addicts, alcoholics, homosexuals, and the clinic. On occasions the words are explicit, on occasions reportorial, sometimes sensual, seldom lyric, seldom sophisticated, sometimes an incoherent riot of words tumbling over one another.

But back of all language is an idea, or a mood, or a feeling. Words in themselves are innocent. We should look through the diction of the erotic absurd to the thoughts and feelings that are expressed by the harmless symbols. And what we find, if we are objective, are expressions of disgust, of rage, of guilt and shame, of contempt, of fear, of sickness. It appears, then, that though the diction is emancipated and as we would say often vulgar in the extreme, it is the language of certain moods of modern life; and if today's language of sex is the exaggerated reverse of the way in which sexual behavior used to be talked about in polite literature, that in itself is a comment on our age.

IRONY OF SITUATION

A study of the use of irony from classical antiquity to the

---

[6] It is perhaps important to remember that we should not be prejudiced against all frank writing on the basis of the trash that seems often to follow in the wake of a new direction in art.

present would reveal, I suspect, that western man has ever been surprised to find that experience altogether too often does not correspond in practice to what he thinks in principle it ought to be. But the irony of the absurd is only in part the presentation of the opposite of what one would normally expect should happen; it is more often the brutal intensification of what one fully expects to happen but which ought not to be permitted to happen in any reasonable or just universe at any time, especially if the wishes of mankind are to be taken into consideration. The irony in the novels of Thomas Hardy is nineteenth-century astonishment that misfortune should occur when, as Hardy says in the poem "Hap,"

> These purlind Doomsters had as readily strown
> Blisses about my pilgrimage as pain.

Modern irony, however, only convinces us of what we already suspected, that, even though it is an ill wind that blows nobody good, circumstance is no more a friend to man than roulette, that values and happenings are at present so thoroughly deranged there is little dependable order in human affairs. It is not the shock of the unexpected that we find in modern irony, but rage at the duplicity of time unfolding in the wrong direction, at the injustice of the *expected*. In an age of little faith, where there is no explanation to absorb the shock of that which should not have happened, the ironic becomes mere fact; and universal anxiety is the issue. When "change" is the major assumption of a social philosophy, then whatever is is right, since whatever happens is consistent with an abstract master plan for the future; but this philosophy has always been cool comfort to most people as they live their everyday lives here and now.

When, in 1918, we read that the sensitive and courageous English poet of World War I, Wilfred Owen, was killed at the Sambre Canal only a week before the signing of the armistice, we recoiled at the irony of fate which is so precise in rendering the opposite of what one would, preferably and with good reason, expect. We called this tragic irony. When we read that Anton Webern, the Austrian composer, a "harmless, gentle man, whose only passions in life were music and flowers," was accidentally shot down in his Mittersill garden during the Allied

107

occupation on September 15, 1945,[7] we are inclined to say that the event was not so much a twist of fate as simply a happening which ought not to have happened. Fate, in other words, is not a turn of the mysterious wheel of fortune; fate is fact. There is no irony where the un-wished-for may be anticipated.

In the older rhetoric, irony inspired philosophic reflection on the meaning for human life of fortuitous incongruities. In modern rhetoric, irony presents the facts of fate wherein the unexpected becomes commonplace, where the unexpected, paradoxically, is the expected. This is the logic of the absurd, that all things tend to contradict themselves; and it is the contradiction that interests us. The absurd, too, calls for speculation on the meaning of life. "To say that life is absurd, the conscience must be alive," says Camus in *The Rebel*. Moreover, "the real nature of the absurd . . . is that it is an experience to be lived through, a point of departure, the equivalent, in existence, of Descartes's methodical doubt." One must start, in other words, from contradiction if he is to find his way to harmony and order.

To many writers of modern imaginative literature that which does not fit into the established scheme of things is not ironic, it is absurd, because irony implies a fate in which there may be method, and the absurd implies an anarchy which *is*. It is the irony of the absurd that the opposite of the established order is expected, exposed, and possibly deplored; but mainly it is to be noted.

We might call it ironic that the thirty-eight-year-old protagonist, Humbert Humbert, in Nabokov's *Lolita* should be taken by uninformed observers to be the father of the cute little twelve-year-old Lolita, when in reality he is her lover. It might be thought of as ironic that Humbert Humbert should be considered a proper parent, when in reality his love for the nymphette Lolita is a psychopathic obsession. But these are not ironies; they are clinical fact.

In Flannery O'Connor's short story, "Good Country People," irony in the older sense is present in that these people are not what they have been expected to be, dependable, respectable,

[7]Andre Hodeir, *Since Debussy: A View of Contemporary Music* (New York, 1961), p. 70.

law-abiding, healthy. They are the opposite. The young man who sells Bibles to the good country people carries preparations in his suitcase (along with a small stock of his product) for any chance or premeditated sexual encounter. Hulga is thirty years old, unmarried, has an artificial leg, reads Malebranche, is sullen and irritable, and lives with her mother on a farm in Georgia. Meeting the Bible salesman one day in her mother's parlor, she plans to seduce him. Later, as Hulga and the young man climb the ladder to the hay loft of the barn, she observes him carrying his suitcase and says, "We won't need the Bible." He replies, "You never can tell." After some unpleasant truths about the young man are revealed during the foreplay, Hulga is astonished to find that it is not herself he wants; it is, rather, her artificial leg, with which presently he makes off, saying, as he disappears through the opening in the loft, "And I'll tell you another thing, Hulga, . . . you ain't so smart. I been believing in nothing ever since I was born!"

The irony of the absurd is here displayed in all its modernity. The incident is not so much ironic as it is an objective correlative of the perverted inner lives of the characters. Obscene, terrifying, this adventure in hypocrisy and perversity is not unexpected. The event is itself not ironic. Character is fate, it has been said; and so it is in the story. Mainly, however, we are assaulted with an explicable event containing some disagreeable news about the way some people behave under certain circumstances. This is not the irony of fate in which a concatenation of happenings has produced a turn to be deplored, nor is the "flaw" in the character of Hulga a necessarily tragic one. It is an existential fact of life.

HYPERBOLE

Hyperbole used as a figure of speech gives boldness and sometimes force to style through expressions of an unnatural or impossible number, magnitude, duration, or condition. When Prince Hal in Shakespeare's *King Henry IV*, Part I, makes fun of Hotspur, he uses mimicry reinforced with exaggeration in terms of number:

Prince. I am not yet of Percy's mind, the Hotspur of the north; he kills me some six or seven dozen of Scots at a breakfast, washes his hands and says to his wife 'Fie upon this quiet life! I want work.' 'O my sweet Harry,' says she, 'how many hast thou killed today?' 'Give my roan horse a drench,' says he; and answers 'Some fourteen,' an hour after; 'a trifle, a trifle.'

Dante's description of Satan in Canto XXXIV of the *Inferno* is forcefully graphic in terms of magnitude:

> The emperor of the dolorous realm
>   from mid-breast protruded from the ice,
>   and I compare in size
> With the giants than they do with his arms.
>   (Trans. H. R. Huse.)

In the English epic *Beowulf*, the hero is unsurpassed in deeds of strength and daring. Here the hyperbole is based on duration, the endurance of the hero exaggerated to the point of impossibility, though not incredibility.[8]

Hyperbole of condition is a most subtle feature of rhetoric, appearing when style and content are closely integrated. For instance, Cleopatra's love for Mark Anthony is the very extremity of love—the condition of love exaggerated beyond what we think of as normally human, though not incredible as Shakespeare tells the story. When Cleopatra kills herself by applying the poisonous snake to her breast, her words, consonant with her character, are mighty indeed. The enormous hyperbole of likening the asp to a baby is one of the richest and most revealing of ironic metaphors used to describe the human condition.[9]

---

[8]Aristotle observes in the *Poetics* that a poet should construct a sequence of events which, "though actually impossible, looks reasonable." This probable impossibility should "be preferred by the poet to what, though really possible, seems incredible." (Trans. Lane Cooper.) It seems to me impossible that any mortal man, as Beowulf, could survive to kill a monster of the sea after the man had been in cold northern waters for five days and nights weighed down by a corselet of heavy mail and burdened for the duration with a battle sword. But if anyone could perform this feat, it was, by definition, Beowulf; and I do not find the exploit incredible. My disbelief is willingly suspended. Achilles, it will be remembered, was also capable of battle strength beyond that of mortal man; but Achilles was a mortal man only on the father's side, and this fact, though unusual, explains in part why Achilles was able to do the things he did.

[9]In melodrama, hyperbole of condition is the main rhetorical ingredient. Since, however, melodrama lacks all else of dramatic power and linguistic skill, it is of a lower order of artistic creation. One cannot help observing,

The hyperbole of the absurd is almost invariably hyperbole of condition, and in one way or another of the human condition of our time. Whereas the older literature often exaggerated the human condition upward, contemporary literature tends to exaggerate the human condition downward. In his fierce indignation Swift could exaggerate the human condition downward to the low level of Yahoos; but he could also elevate it to the high level of Houyhnhnms. There is, however, more to the hyperbole of the absurd than mere eloquence visited upon degeneration.

Samuel Beckett is justly one of the famous playwrights of the absurd. *Endgame,* for example, is a riddle in the form of an extended hyperbole of the human condition.[10] From the dialogue and the setting, we gather that the four characters of the play, Hamm, the central figure; Clov, his sometimes rebellious but mostly obedient servant; Nell and Nagg, mother and father of Hamm, are the only people on the earth. The time is not the dawn of the first day when the morning stars sang together but the twilight of the last where there are no stars at all. In the beginning, God created the Heaven and the earth. At the end, according to St. John the Divine, God destroyed the world and the wicked with it. "And he said unto me. It is done. I am Alpha and Omega, the beginning and the end." (Revelation, 21,6.) In the beginning there was the Garden of Eden; at the end there is the cellar refuge—an ark without hope. Between the Alpha and Omega multitudinous human beings have suffered through the millennia as though there had been no beginning and would be no end. In *Endgame,* Beckett has had the audacity to bring the world to a close, a monstrous hyperbole

---

for instance, that Richard Wagner was not, in the literary medium, successful in the creation of the character of Siegfried, a hero of proportions quite beyond belief. I can more readily believe that Hecuba in her agony should bark like a dog than that Siegfried could understand the language of the birds. But Richard Wagner was not a literary genius. He was a musical genius, and he used musical hyperbole (if the phrase is permissible) to create characters larger than life with a success at which we can only marvel that the world should have such composers in it.

[10]The rhetoric of the absurd does not use hyperbole for display, as an ornament of style designed to stimulate the reader's attention, but rather as a riddle which presents a condition with the utmost intensity. "Good metaphors can usually be made from successful riddles, for metaphors are a kind of riddle." Aristotle, *Rhetoric,* Grube translation.

111

but not an incredible one. He has dared to isolate four people in a cavernous shelter, to put two of them, Nell and Nagg, in garbage cans, and to fashion in a few pages of text a cosmic drama in the form of a summing up of those millennia between the Alpha and the Omega. This concentration of the summing up is in itself a bold exaggeration, a modern hyperbole in the hands of a master of dramatic art.

Great authors have often portrayed the human condition in allegory that depends for its power on imaginative hyperbole. The *Holy Bible*, Dante, Milton, Goethe tried their skill at cosmic drama. Whereas in the earlier writers the story closes with anthem upon anthem to the glory of the divine, refreshing us with hope of wonders to come, the modern hyperbole is a cry of anguish at the center of the void. There is, however, in *Endgame*, one consolation. There is the handkerchief, "Old Stancher." It remains, the blood-stained symbol of suffering which covers and hides the agony, the only improvisation of which man is capable on his own, the game of covering one's wounds and of waiting.

This is all very extreme. But it is the purpose of art to concentrate, that is, to exaggerate, and Beckett has concentrated centuries of proud intellection into a few moments of intense futility and despair. *Endgame* is monstrous, if one takes it literally, which one should not do, of course, remembering that it is an ingenious metaphor of metaphysical anguish. It is not possible for art to be nihilistic, and Beckett's art is far from nihilistic. Here is the human condition, A.D. 1950, raised to a pitch of artistic intensity which for that reason if for no other makes it positive and gives it meaning and status.

METAPHOR

Though respect for "reason" as we ordinarily understand its application in human affairs has had its ups and downs, sometimes suspect, sometimes elevated, now retiring, now resurgent, historically it seems to have been the foundation for what we call civilized society. But human reason is not, as we often suppose, a mere putting of two and two together or even a method of solving problems by way of detached observation. In classical

Greece it was expressed not in answers and decisions but in the Apollonian ideals of harmony, cosmos, order, and the middle way of "nothing too much." In Augustan Rome it was articulated in just legal codes and in the literary ideals of correctness, taste, refinement. In the eighteenth century it was the noblest effort of the mind, related to political theory, philosophical inquiry, and scientific investigation.

In the twentieth century, reason has suffered greatly at the hands of unreason. The last appearance of reason in full panoply may have been in the 1930s, that is, in England and America; for since 1940 (in spite of Henry Adams's pious hope) not even the most determined of optimists, it seems, can look at the contemporary world without a shudder.

In the concluding pages of his book *A Hope for Poetry* (1934), C. Day Lewis says:

> It is . . . the nature of the poetic imagination to become aware of the cryptic links that bind our universe together, to find similarity in difference and to make coherence out of contradiction.

Mainly, the sensibility of the younger poets of the 1930s, for example W. H. Auden and Stephen Spender, was marked by sensitivity to change, sensitivity to the new, the determination to be "modern." Their purpose was to observe and record but at the same time to transform information into patterns of unity, to make coherence out of contradiction.

In his autobiographical *World Within World*, Stephen Spender speaks of "the modern consciousness of politics as a universal fate." He himself was "political," he says, not just because he was involved, but because he felt he must choose to defend a good cause against a bad one. And Spender recalls that Auden had remarked to him at the end of the war that he was political in the 1930s "because he thought something could and should be done." The writers of the 1930s wished to be clear-eyed and rational, to see into the historic moment, to name its defects, and to do something about them on the basis of a logic which "must choose to defend a good cause against a bad one." This new sensibility was, it seems now, the last sign of reason in a war-torn world.

It is possible, instead, that the language of the irrational may be the only language in which to talk about the patterns of disunity in our time, about the contrarieties and inconsistencies in a world that is supposed to be rational.

In 1944, a novel by Charles Jackson entitled *The Lost Weekend* quickly became a bestseller. *The Lost Weekend* discloses the intimate thoughts and behavior of an incurable alcoholic whose name is Don Birnam. The book is sufficiently clinical so as to be a convincing picture of dipsomania. For one reason or another, the person addicted to alcohol *prefers* to see the world as it appears to a brain controlled by a system that has a large quantity of alcohol in it. The "natural" way of seeing the world is the way most people see it when they are sober, at least this is what most people assume; and it is the "natural" way because a number of sober people will agree, if only roughly, on what they see.

To the poet A. E. Housman, the "real" world is the world of the sober eye; and when we "Look into the pewter pot," we see the world "as the world's not." Interestingly, however, to see the world as the world's not is upon occasions the desire of "normal" curiosity. But the curiosity is based on the firm belief that the world is not really the way it looks to the eye under the influence of alcohol. Occasional looking into the pewter pot is indulged on the guarantee that the outer world will remain what it is, that it can be returned to, like a dependable home, at any time one wishes. It is impossible to imagine what existence would be if the opposite were the case, if most people were intoxicated (i.e., under the influence of alcohol) most of the time, and some were sober some of the time. The experience of momentary sobriety would be the experience of an incredible revelation.

What fascinated readers of *The Lost Weekend* when it was first published may have been the glimpse it afforded of the mind of the compulsive drinker; and it appears that Birnam was driven to drink, so that for the duration of his intoxication he might be relieved of the feelings of guilt and shame with which he is tormented in his sober moments.

There is, however, much more to the novel than the report of an alcoholic weekend. The book may be read as an extended figure of speech, an allegory of our time. It is a metaphor of intoxication and of the irrational that is intrinsic to it. In order to quiet the feelings of guilt and shame that seem, like the Furies, to pursue us, we turn to the intoxicant, whatever it may be, and to the irrational view of life which it inspires. The intoxicant may be anything—from alcohol to status, to sex, to power (liquor, love, and fights, as A. E. Housman put it).

One of the scenes in the novel is the account of a characteristic hallucination of delirium tremens. As he lies in bed suffering from the withdrawal of alcohol from his system, Birnam sees a mouse come out of a hole in the wall near the ceiling. Though as a rule he is afraid of mice, he takes at that moment a fellow-sufferer's interest in the frightened creature. Then, flying so close to Birnam's head as to brush his temple with its wing, a bat attacks the mouse and Birnam watches in horror the mortal combat which ensues. The struggle of the bat and the mouse is a literary scene with symbolic significance. The terror is inspired by an imaginary event for the purpose of making more vivid the real feelings of guilt and remorse which pursue the victim, as the Furies pursue Orestes in *The Eumenides* of Aeschylus.

In other words, the hallucination produced by the delirium is, in the hands of the writer, a metaphor of the absurd because it is not really happening and yet it is there all the same. The battle of the bat and the mouse was real enough to the protagonist, fierce and obscene, but to Helen, sympathetic friend and nurse caring for the sick Birnam, there was no hole in the wall, no mouse, no bat—"and she was right," says the author. The event is a literary metaphor of interior anguish and torment.

Metaphors of the irrational are to be found in much absurdist literature. To see the world as the world's not can be induced temporarily through alcohol but permanently through power madness, suffering, poverty, humiliation, violence.

* * * * *

It is tempting to find in the literature of the absurd a "new reason," paradoxical as that now seems. In support of this idea, recall that in the *Oresteia* of Aeschylus only Athena could put an end to the blood-vengeance of the Furies. The Furies are a metaphor of the irrational. Only Athena could look upon the horrid creatures and not blench; only reason, for which she stands, could persuade and transform them into a force for the good. The new reason, embodied in Athena, is, in the *Oresteia,* the power of arbitration. In the philosophy of the absurd, the new reason does not flinch at inconsistencies (incongruities, paradoxes, opposites, image within contrary image, unreal within real) but faces the irrational with the will to arbitrate among the conflicting forces of life and experience, to reconcile the pattern of the "boarhound and the boar."

When finally the Chorus of Furies accepts Athena's offer of goodwill and a place beside her in Athens, she says:

> Zeus, king of parley, doth prevail,
> And ye and I will strive nor fail,
>   That good may stand in evil's stead,
> And lasting bliss for bale.
>   (Trans. E. D. A. Morshead.)

Language and Truth

L EARNING to call things by the names that general agreement has bestowed upon them is an elementary exercise of the mind, one which we associate with the education of small children. The first step in teaching a child to talk usually consists of a fond parent's pointing to an object and repeating a word, such as "cow," or "horse," or "dog." The purpose of this exercise is, of course, to teach the child to connect the word with the thing. And when finally the little one himself points with his finger and says, "cow," the happy parents applaud with pardonable pride. It is thus that the learning process proceeds—with the picture books that make cows so very cowlike, with trains, automobiles, and other readily available vehicles, with edible substances, with heat and cold, with the names of aunts and uncles, and so on. As we know from this experience with children, the mere accumulation of name-words is but a beginning, a first faltering, unsure step toward knowledge.

There are some people who, intellectually at least, never seem to rise above or go beyond the mere naming of things, which for them constitutes knowledge, even truth. We all remember how when we were small boys and girls we had a playmate whose irritating business it was to learn by heart the names of certain objects, such as those which make up the equipment and parts of sail boats, the substance and manufacture of marbles, or the terminology used in dress-making, or the names for tools in a carpenter's shop, and who turned the conversation whenever possible (which was most of the time) upon the subjects he knew so well, tense in argument over whether this was a this or a that, and hilarious when he caught you in error, maddening because he was so often right.

Unhappily, this pride in so low an order of mental activity may be found in adults in varying degrees of intensity. That man is not hard to find who has studied up in advance of an occasion the names for things which are bound to become a considerable part of the conversation. Inevitably he will bring the talk around to what he has studied to remember—statistics, perhaps, the population of a certain city, some odd detail which *you* would have to ransack your memory for (providing you had time, which of course you never do); or he will engage you in conversation about the names of plants or animals or machines and their parts, or certain facts to be discovered from looking at maps, like distances between villages, or perchance dates (where he can be exasperatingly correct), like 1066 A.D., or even, indeed, the names of musical compositions or the titles of paintings, usually those of the old masters (Rembrandt particularly has been chosen for this sort of idle entertainment), and so on *ad nauseam*.

Now to be sure, a knowledge of names is indispensable in the struggle of the human race for survival. We all like to feel certain that when we ask the druggist for aspirin, we shall get aspirin and not bichloride of mercury tablets. We depend with a childlike faith on names, that they will go with that which we have been taught to expect them to go with. And in the higher reaches of thought, in the physical and biological sciences, a classification is a meaningful arrangement, and names become tools without which civilization, to say nothing of human thought itself, would be very nearly impossible. Yet even here one can be misled into thinking he knows something when he doesn't. Unless one has some kind of plan or purpose for the use of his knowledge, some imagination, in short, the memorization of names can be a waste of time.

When I was an undergraduate, I used to help my roommate, who was a forestry student, with his study of *Gray's Manual of Botany*. We had our taxonomic hours once a week when I would hear him recite from memory the divisions, the orders, the families, the genera, and the species of the flowering plants and ferns treated in the seventh edition of *Gray's Manual*. To this day I remember the names of some of the families, the rose family, for instance, which is called Rosaceae; the pulse family, Leguminosae; the beech family, Fagaceae (which I enjoyed hearing about more than many of the others as it had to do with trees I particularly admired—the beech, the chestnut, and the oak). But since at the time I speak of, these fearfully learned names (established by international congresses of botanists) meant nothing to me, and as I had no use to put them to, I knew the names only as prodigious to spell and for the most part ludicrous to hear. To a plant scientist, the name Lentibulariaceae (bladderwort family) is something he keeps to himself, seldom venturing it upon a lay company. With men of true learning—in the sciences, in the humanities, in the professions—the using of names with precision is a mark of skill and the result of long training.

If the using of names with precision within the context of an occupation is of a higher order of mind than mere information as to the names of things, then the making up of names, the giving of names to things, requires real creative ability. Naming a continent (Africa, Asia, America) would be a grave responsibility and would, I should think, call for a poet, or someone, at any rate, with an active, rich, and philosophic imagination. Consider the pain (though not perhaps depth of imagination) that often accompanies the naming of children and how in older times a contemplative working of the mind must have been required to suggest those Mercys and Charitys and Hepzibahs. Indeed, the giving of names summons up now a fine technique, now philosophic insight, now the folk wisdom of a people. It takes learning and understanding to give names to trees—for instance, the Judas tree, blushing as it does a pale pink in the spring, the Woman's Tongue tree of tropical climes with its clusters of dry pods that chatter in the slightest breeze. How were the names Hibiscus and Oleander arrived at as names for the shrubs they signify? Who decided upon Magnolia and Holly, and how did the Algonquins come to fancy Tamarack for the American Larch? The names of flowers, plants, and herbs are often richly suggestive, and, in time, after long association with what they stand for, become haunting and lovely: the Damask Rose (which Katherine Anne Porter says was the first recorded name of a rose), the Musk Rose, the yellow Eglantine, the Cup of Hebe—Tansy, Feverfew, Nightshade, Hyssop, Lavender, Monkshood, Foxglove, Rue.

Think at what a loss one would be to have to fancy names

of places like Saranac, Capri, Madagascar, Paris, Soho, Damascus, or even Londonderry and Vermont. Tools have astonishing names, and one cannot but wonder who it was who told first how they should be called: awl, scythe, capstan, jackknife, colander. And what a brave world is it that hath in it such names as cashmere, velvet, cambric, canvas, silk, and chiffon. Naming the stars was no child's play, and now that we have them fixed who would venture to say whether they could be better named: Orion, Aldebaran, the Pleiades, the Hyades. And one would have to climb Parnassus more than half way to fashion names for the gods—Tammuz, Osiris, Dionysus, Apollo. What a noble work of man, this making of names to stand for all the things of this various world, the things that can be seen and touched, and worked with, and names, too, for all the insubstantial pageants of the mind.

If the learning of names is an elementary exercise of the mind, the learning of facts is scarcely more, though as with naming, the learning of facts is another step in the direction of truth and can be made up of richly satisfying lessons. Most human being have an instinct for facts, for those facts, at any rate, which it is profitable for them to have an instinct for. We often surprise an aura of truth shining through facts; and it is perhaps our own discovery of facts that means most to us educationally.

But one has to be wary. What are facts? Facts are not, it seems, always facts. Things are not always what they are *said* to be. Let us suppose that we are walking in a museum and that we stop before a painting that suddenly demands our attention. On the frame at the bottom is printed in black letters the name of a famous painter, Botticelli for instance. Let us suppose further that we are students of art appreciation and are so pleased with our discovery that we tell it to our teacher. Our teacher, being a knowledgeable person, replies that he is acquainted with the painting, that it is such and such a style, but that it is really "contemporary Botticelli." In other words, the painting was not done by Botticelli himself but by someone "of the school of Botticelli," one of the master's students perhaps. Our teacher informs us that many paintings whose artists are unknown but which are typical of a master are said to belong to a school and often carry the name of the painter whose style, etc., they so closely resemble. If one of us has the temerity to observe that since it is not a fact that Botticelli painted the picture, his name should not be attached to it, our teacher may well reply that if we like the picture and it says something to us, what difference does it make (except to professional art historians) who painted the picture.

In our hypothetical case, it has now become necessary to dismiss from our minds the name of the painter of the picture as irrelevant. Instead, our interest lies in certain critical refinements and niceties of explanation as make a statement of fact not a statement of fact. Often, it seems, we are less interested in "facts" and more interested in what we say about them, and consequently, it is the talking about them that becomes important. We refine upon the so-called facts, modify and color them, put them on condition and make them provisional.

Yet certain facts are so persistent that they will not knuckle under—the facts one works with, for instance. A poem by Robert Frost entitled "Mowing" comes spontaneously to my mind, especially the last six lines:

> Anything more than the truth would have seemed too weak
> To the earnest love that laid the swale in rows,
> Not without feeble-pointed spikes of flowers
> (Pale orchises), and scared a bright green snake.
> The fact is the sweetest dream that labor knows.
> My long scythe whispered and left the hay to make.

It is a commonplace, of course, that Americans are a practical people (not caring enough, perhaps, for the imaginative and speculative), with a long heritage of faith in facts. That the early puritans were a practical band of pilgrims is well known. Though they toiled in the wilderness to build a Holy Commonwealth, still they had a considerable regard for the practical affairs of everyday life. The church had its awe-inspiring words, but the wood-pile was a fact of life. Not a few of our steeple-crowned forebears would have agreed quite readily with the Connecticut Yankee in Rose Terry Cooke's novel *Steadfast*, who says: "At heart every human being has the infidelity of the Apostle Thomas hidden in some shadowy recess, where it whis-

pers to itself, 'I will not believe what I do not see and touch.'"
Even Emerson the idealist paid his respects to the hard facts on
many an occasion:

> Bulkeley, Hunt, Willard, Hosmer, Meriam, Flint,
> Possessed the land which rendered to their toil
> Hay, corn, roots, hemp, flax, apples, wool and wood.

Though it is in the realm of the moral and spiritual that we
expect to find the abiding *abstract* truths, there where the mason-
ry of accumulated facts has been transformed into the ideal design, nevertheless it is to the concrete everyday facts, objects of
use and beauty and wonder—the inorganic earth substances, and
air and fire and water, all the growing things of the earth and all
the living creatures, all the people of the earth, and the works of
their hands and minds, and the records of all their lives—it is to
these that we turn for reassurance of the reality of the world and
for support of our endeavors in it. One does well to hold
fast to "facts" as firm friends to go by his side in the pursuit of
the higher truths.

In the Ford Times Special Edition (Number 2) *New England Journeys,* there is a short piece by William Faulkner called
"A Guest's Impression of New England." In this little appreciation Mr. Faulkner tells a revealing story. "One afternoon," he
says, "(it was October, the matchless Indian summer of New
England) Malcolm Cowley and I were driving through back
roads in western Connecticut and Massachusetts. We got lost
. . . The road was not getting worse yet: just hillier and lonelier
and apparently going nowhere save upward, toward a range of
hills. At last, just as we were going to turn back, we found a
house, a mailbox, two men, farmers or in the costume of farmers
. . . standing beside the mailbox, and watching us quietly and
with perfect courtesy as we drove up and stopped.

"'Good afternoon,' Cowley said.

"'Good afternoon,' one of the men said.

"'Does this road cross the mountain?' Cowley said.

"'Yes,' the man said, still with that perfect courtesy.

"'Thank you,' Cowley said and drove on, the two men still
watching us quietly—for perhaps fifty yards, when Cowley
braked suddenly and said, 'Wait,' and backed the car down to

the mailbox again where the two men still watched us. 'Can I get over it in this car?' Cowley said.

"'No,' the same man said. 'I don't think you can.' So we turned around and went back the way we came."

Most of us spend most of our time getting and giving information. Certain pieces of information are basic to survival, the "where it is and how to get it" kind, and for the most part this simple information is readily available if we care to make use of it. Indeed, it is the purpose of the social order to make information available, and fortunately certain pieces (such as vital statistics) are required by law to be published. But in the socially less well-regulated affairs (or socially not regulated at all) information is by no means easy to come by or necessarily known or understood though it might stare one in the face. The location of an unknown oil deposit takes time and skill to find; if one really loses a twenty-dollar bill, information as to its whereabouts is impossible to get; if criminals wanted by the police are successful in hiding out against the law, information about them may be available, but it is not forthcoming; if one wants to know what the future movement of certain stocks is going to be, he has to have information which is apparently very difficult for the average man to find and, if achieved, is not always reliable anyway. Though actuarial tables will predict the probable length of your life, absolute information about your longevity is nowhere to be had. Information as to whether one has achieved salvation is, mostly, I believe, a jealously guarded secret; information about whether one is really loved is often singularly difficult to draw out; information about one's future prospects, though it *may* lie in the palm of one's hand, is by no means infallible even if offered; information about the plans of one's enemies can be got, but it is not always trustworthy and often requires such delicate interpretation that most of us lack the key required for decoding the messages. Then again, what passes for information today may turn out to be but opinion tomorrow—to emend Henry Thoreau. Dependable information about the nature of the physical world, about the universe and universes at large, is mighty hard to come by, though

123

of course physicists and astronomers lay claim now and then to the receipt of valuable disclosures.

When we try to find out information about ourselves, we are altogether too often at a loss which way to turn. The doctor cannot always tell us what is wrong with us, nor can the psychiatrist. Information about oneself is very nearly the hardest information to get and may require the sufferings of Oedipus and a lifetime to achieve. Our "selves" lie buried deep, like hidden treasures, and the maps we have drawn up about ourselves are not so easy to follow as those we have made of the public highways.

Because we know so little about ourselves, or because the information we have got is so garbled, we have to ask ourselves over and over again what our conduct should be in this or that predicament. Where can we learn how to behave? There are books in abundance, there is the law, there are other people who will suggest the rules for our conduct. For want of dependable information, we often resort to what the Existentialists call "role-playing." We learn the kind of conduct expected of a person who engages in our kind of activity, and we try to behave according to the stereotype established for that activity. Information about how to play a role is helpful in a complicated society, but following it to the letter is, after all, denying one's own uniqueness and cutting one's self to the common pattern.

Except for downright dangerous indifference to accurate information (say the information on labels in a drug store), we tend to believe what we want to believe. So deeply embedded in us is the will to believe what it suits us at the moment to believe that we stand in need of constant correction, of being corrected by others around us who do not cherish the same illusions as we do. Curiously, it is easy to believe what one wants to believe. Facts are not so stubborn and brutal as we have been led to think, and one can get information which will support his wishful thinking without much trouble. Misinterpreting information is a common enough practice, but wilful perversion or misconstruction of information is a daily strategy. Deep inner desires will cause outward facts to suffer rare changes; wanting things desperately enough will change the face of reality altogether, so that what *seems* and what *is* become two different realities. Sophistical or false interpretation of factual information colors ethics, judgment, taste. As our desires become more intense, we tend wilfully to alter, in our minds, the nature of the world around us.

When Prospero in *The Tempest* tells Miranda how his brother, the false Antonio, usurped his dukedom, it was because, Prospero says, he had given Antonio too much trust, and too much power, so that being thus lorded

> Not only with what my revenue yielded,
> But what my power might else exact, like one
> Who having into truth, by telling of it,
> Made such a sinner of his memory,
> To credit his own lie, he did believe
> He was indeed the duke.

Because information about anything beyond the time of day or one's neighbor's telephone number often requires such toil to secure, is often unreliable, and often, also, so set with thorns, true information is one of the most precious of man's acquisitions and the purpose of all his searching. Is it any wonder that information is power? We make a great effort to share certain kinds of information, the discoveries and findings of medicine, for example; unshared information, military secrets for instance, can be used as a weapon, giving the owner unimaginable power and profit. There are times when we have some but not all the necessary information; there are times when we are not willing to give up the information we have; now and then we are unwilling to receive information, if it is of a kind painful to us; and there are many instances where we do not know how to go about getting information. This explains why education today is devoted almost exclusively to the principles for procuring information, is devoted to skills and training in the use of instruments designed to extract information from intractable and obstinate sources.

The most accurate and dependable information we have for practical daily use is achieved through the techniques and principles of research developed by modern science in all its branches. And modern science has built up an enormous body of information which it is constantly measuring, sifting, and interpreting, so that it may be made applicable in human affairs. Since the seventeenth century, the people of the western world have looked to science for information about the world; and science, as a method of investigation, has proved miraculously successful and effective.

If knowledge of naming and of facts, if the accumulation of information and the testing and weighing of it are the materials of learning, creative use of the materials, as in the making of judgments and the finding of truths is the final goal of learning—that is, of an education. It is of judgment and truth that I should like to speak in the remainder of this essay.

The formation of value judgments takes time—more time, usually, than we feel we can give, in this workaday world. As a matter of fact, centuries may be required to sift the best from all the many contenders in all the fields of human experience—in social institutions, in political thought, in literature and the arts, as well as in French cooking. Time, we say, is the judge, but time has always needed allies, generations of human beings whose wish is to be civilized. Perhaps the most important part of all higher education is the learning to discriminate, to distinguish among all things to find that which is best and most worthy to be preserved. The monuments of a civilization survive because, after long acquaintance with them, a people have valued them worthiest of survival, have found them lasting in value and worthy of preservation. There is a difference between a crab apple and an orchard apple (as I believe John Burroughs, the naturalist, once pointed out), between a just government and a tyrannical one, between the *Iliad* and hundreds of forgotten war novels written since the time of Homer. And the difference between these examples is not quite a matter of personal taste, despite the theory of cultural relativity. It is very real, as most people know.

As with the gathering of information, the making of judgments is often conditioned by prejudice toward those judgments which it will benefit us personally to make. Objectivity is a rare talent and always has been. Wishful thinking often dictates what we shall like and hold good. If our interests are at stake (and in matters of taste our *feelings* are certainly involved), we *can* prefer the monstrous to the beautiful and good. All the subtle demands of vanity and self-interest, of the ego studying to be heard in the world, tend to make our judgments deeply subjective. But who can say absolutely what is good and what is beautiful?

How shall we learn to judge? How shall we judge, for instance, the value of a work of art? What standards shall we employ? At this point I shall certainly disappoint some of my readers. I cannot give the answer ready-made; for if I could, there would have been little purpose in the thoughts I have thus far labored to bring forth. Fashions change, fads come and go, but somehow through that drop-by-drop process known as education, the superior things remain and serve as touchstones for the future. To emend the Spanish philosopher Jose Ortega y Gasset, it is the daily plebiscite of civilized people carrying the vote for the best that makes the best survive. The formation of taste is not alone a matter of learning the rules. It is rather more a matter of immersing oneself in that which has been tried and found good, in the accumulated body of judgments of the people of a culture. It is the purpose of higher education, and the purpose of the humane studies especially, to help all students to learn to distinguish between that which is good and that which is not so good, so that they may participate in the universal judging of the best. It is the price of civilization that people must evaluate and re-evaluate, else a culture will fall into a state of maximum mediocrity. And if we tremble and grow faint before the task of making the great judgment, of judging, that is, between good and evil, it is no wonder, since this task has plagued mankind from the beginning of time. But we know only too well that we cannot surrender, nor even despair.

"You are too fond of your liberty," said Mrs. Touchett to her niece, Isabel, in Henry James' *Portrait of a Lady.* "Yes, I think I am very fond of it," Isabel replied. "But I always want to know the things one shouldn't do." "So as to do them?" asked her aunt. "So as to choose," said Isabel.

So as to choose—not only between right and wrong among the strictly moral issues, but among all the multitudes of ideas of our time. And that is where, in our time especially, the agitation lies—in determining what to choose, surrounded as we are by such abundance, such unimaginable plenty, not only in material goods and things, but in ideas, theories, possible beliefs. We enjoy a feast of notions, that is, more probably then we need. Our world of ideas is like an enormous department store where we move idly from counter to counter, trying to decide what we should like to have and whether we can afford the intellectual purchases we might make—for there are entanglements in the big purchases. For one thing we may have to keep up the payments; and in any event we have to protect our prizes from thieves and destroyers. Moths creep into ideas, too. Shall we put all our intellectual and emotional savings into something that will rust when exposed to a little damp air? Sometimes we toy with gewgaws or with the trinkets laid out in an inviting display. We wander through the bargain basement among the cheaper thoughts, those that may serve for a time. Some notions take our fancy, the work of far romantic places and peoples, ideals which have grown up in other cultures than our own. Toward some ideas we are curious, are not sure, and we entertain mingled feelings about them. Toward some we are detached and critical. For some notions we have no use at all, and we hardly see them. Toward some we are attentive; some, in the light, spacious higher galleries, we behold with rapture.

And what shall we wish to save and to keep permanently after we have brought our purchases home and viewed them in a more sober moment; for we shall have to decide sooner or later what to keep and what to throw away. I venture to say that if ever we bring ourselves to make the final choices, we shall discover that they are very simple ones—the image of a landscape that speaks of all the possibilities of freedom; the possession of a love that is all-consuming; the ripening knowledge of what a great poem is saying; the daily revelations of a work of art; the full possession of a disciplined mind; the words of a philosopher that never diminish in their power to help us; the music that does not diminish in its power to move us; the infinite satisfactions of a great religious belief; a noble friendship; a wholly unselfish way of life. But it must be remembered that all these are choices which when we have made them have ruled out the many other possibilities; and it is therefore incumbent upon us to select with the greatest care, lest through ignorance we let the prizes slip through our fingers, remembering also (as E. M. Forster says in his essay "What I Believe") that "there lies at the back of every creed something terrible and hard for which the worshipper may one day be required to suffer."

Anyone who has the temerity to speak of "truth" usually finds that he is performing verbal dances around the *word* truth, rather than letting truth perform for itself. The truth is as hard to talk about as it is to tell, though it is not, I think, so hard to find as people say, nor so ready with a dusty answer. If there is one thing certain, the truth will not be caught *once and for all* in a net of words alone, nor does it like to be imprisoned in a theory; it is much too fond of its liberty. At the outset of any inquiry into the nature of truth, one has, in my opinion, to begin with "facts," that is, with things themselves.

The gross material facts of the world are ready at hand for use in giving mode to the truths drawn from the well of being; and literature and art and history and philosophy and science are the crafts that shape the disembodied truth and make it concrete. Observe how music gives measure to *time,* how painting and architecture and sculpture inform *space,* how history gives a scheme to *past* and *present,* how science makes arrangement of *cause* and *effect,* how philosophy builds the structure of *thought* and literature makes epiphanies of vague *justice, beauty,* and *love.* And do not mistake that the toil exacted to tell the truth is more prodigious than the labors of Hercules, more passing strange, more abundant of enemies and frustration, more unlikely of adjournment. But it is to literature and particularly to the art of poetry that in closing I would turn now, well aware that the same justice might be done the sciences and all the humane studies.

Sun, gold, light, queens, flame, dawn, heart, moon, tears, fields, time, mountains, darkness, wind, the sea, gardens, lions, trees, home, dreams, night, roses, the grave, stars, nightingales— these veritables have been the substance of poetry for a very long time, sense experiences used to express by proxy the thoughts and feelings that are the imaginative life. Every now and then someone cries out against them as overworked and worn out. It is not so much that they are overworked, for they are indefatigable; it is rather that they backslide and refuse to work for some masters. Though the rose, for instance, may have become commonplace in our gardens (as well as in poetry), it is still a flower whose charms are inexhaustible. The rose by no means appeals to all poets in the same way. Each poet will request it to carry *his* message. But like the dawn, and fire, and darkness, and the sea, the rose is always accommodating, if the poet is well-intentioned toward it.

> O, my luve is like a red, red rose
> That's newly sprung in June,

sang Robert Burns. Roses are lovely and so are young Highland girls. The poet was moved by the analogy that spoke unhesitatingly to him as appropriate and true. With A. E. Housman, roses mostly fade—in fields where "rose-lipt girls are sleeping." With T. S. Eliot the rose is self-conscious, at least the roses of "Burnt Norton" have "the look of flowers that are looked at." And Gertrude Stein, bored, perhaps, with antique similitudes, or indignant with the age-long using of the rose as servant to help any poet on with his singing-robes, will have it that "the rose is a rose," only itself with its own life.

The common object is known in its immanence, but not until it is touched by the hand of poetic metaphor is it informed and made vivid with the rich garments of thought and feeling. The metaphor of poetry redeems the thing itself, saves it from being the clod and lump mere use and wont have made of it. Finally, however, it is in the design which the chosen objects make that the truth is realized and becomes a firm and permanent truth of the world, a truth not made but rather "discovered" by the poet, a truth perpetually verified by the experience of mankind.

> *Fame* is the spur that the clear spirit doth raise
> (That last infirmity of Noble mind)
> To scorn delights, and live laborious days;
> But the fair Guerdon when we hope to find,
> And think to burst out into sudden blaze,
> Comes the blind *Fury* with th'abhorred shears,
> And slits the thin spun life. But not the praise,
> *Phoebus* repli'd, and touch'd my trembling ears;

Fame is no plant that grows on mortal soil,
Nor in the glistering foil
Set off to th' world, nor in broad rumour lies,
But lives and spreads aloft by those pure eyes,
And perfect witness of all-judging *Jove;*
As he pronounces lastly on each deed,
Of so much fame in Heav'n expect thy meed.

An abstract *Fame* has here in the hands of Milton become a poetic fact and a massive truth.

But eventually even the poet has to confess that

Words strain,
Crack and sometimes break, under the burden,
Under the tension, slip, slide, perish,
Decay with imprecision, will not stay in place,
Will not stay still.

(T. S. Eliot, "Burnt Norton")

From the last and highest promontory of time, we may see that the truth is not made up of words at all, only that we have had to use words to lure it from its hiding places. And after all is said, it may be (if we can *know* what this means) that the truth is not more than being itself, innocent, eternal being.

But here and now we are obliged to use language and human thought with which to draw up our agreement with reality. Truth is the name we give to the highest and deepest insights, the fruit of long experience, to those ideas and phenomena which have stood the test of our straining at them, which we have judged most likely to endure, which are universally human, and about which disagreement is only inconsequential quibbling.

Unfortunately, the wish for power is sometimes greater than the wish for truth. People sometimes invent the "truth" where it suits them to do so. And sometimes the "truth" seems to be whatever strong and powerful men say it is, and we are stampeded into thinking something is true that deep within us we know is not. The work of our time which deals most commandingly with the wilful perversion of truth is George Orwell's *Nineteen Eighty-Four*. "You believe that reality is something objective," says the novel's Party leader, O'Brien, something "external, existing in its own right." O'Brien is talking to Winston Smith, the unregenerate believer in the ultimate victory of truth and humanity over power and the Party. O'Brien refers to Winston Smith sarcastically as "the last man." He says to him:

> When you delude yourself into thinking that you see something, you assume that everyone else sees the same thing as you. But I tell you, Winston, that reality is not external. Reality exists in the human mind, nowhere else. Not in the individual mind, which can make mistakes, and in any case soon perishes; only in the mind of the Party, which is collective and immortal. Whatever the Party holds to be the truth *is* truth. It is impossible to see reality except by looking through the eyes of the Party. That is the fact that you have got to relearn, Winston. It needs an act of self-destruction, an effort of the will.

Winston Smith withstands as long as he can the torture and the degradation. He insists heroically that reality is not a matter of power and propaganda. Men are not "infinitely malleable." "There is something in the universe . . . some spirit, some principle . . . that the power-mad will never overcome."

That spirit, that principle, is the indifferent, innocent truth, indifferent, that is, to parties and politics, by nature incapable of self-corruption. It is that which we are a part of and is a part of us, that which is ours as well as everyone else's; it is individualistic as well as communal, the possession of all people, like life and hunger and time, self-evident like fire and air and one's personality, inhabiting space, yet individually experienced as wholly and legitimately one's own, which cannot be gainsaid, short of bitter divorce between the nature of the world and human thought. For human thought searches out the closest possible correspondence between things in the outside world and our inner understanding of them, it seeks (with a hopefulness which if it were naive would be intolerable mockery) the near-perfect adaptation of a sane intellect to a sane world. And that is why the human perversion of even the smallest truths strikes us as perilous, and why the perversion of the massive truths is unforgiveable. One may well shake one's head with George Eliot's puzzled Mr. Tulliver over the thought that a perfectly sane intellect is hardly at home in an insane world—is hardly at home, that is, in a world made insane by those who, power hungry, prefer darkness to light.

Metaphor and Beyond

I

THE LANGUAGE that represents the facts of our world may be called "the language of reports." The language of reports refers directly to objects and events and is not purposely evaluative or conceptual. It is the language that attaches words to visible things for the purpose of identifying them and their relationship to one another and to human beings. It coincides closely with human experience in the world. It is the language that gives information without judgment, that invites no presuppositions, permits of no prejudice, is in itself incorruptible, and is, therefore, vital to the survival of humanity. It is the language that refreshes the mind and keeps us in touch with reality. It is the language of children as well as of the most learned men. It is the language of names, where we try for universal agreement. A book, rose oil, a locust tree, a moth, peppermint candy, a jackknife, a McIntosh apple, wormwood, a pigeon, majolica pottery, New York City — these are things we can know directly with our senses.

The language of reports can be learned and used, accurately or inaccurately. It is a communal style, and its meaning is the sharing of information for the public good. For example, the language of *The Pharmacopœia of the United States* represents an organization of knowledge which is in the public domain. There is in this work a universally agreed upon and reliable vocabulary and a universally agreed upon arrangement of words. The *Pharmacopœia* is cast in a style which has for its sole purpose the unambiguous communication of dependable information.

The language of reports is not limited to statements of everyday fact. It is the language of much of medical literature, of natural history, of botany, of travel, of history, of anthropology. It is the language of the classics in these fields, of Sir William Osler's *The Principles and Practice of Medicine,* of Charles M. Doughty's *Travels in Arabia Deserta,* of Charles Darwin's *The Voyage of the Beagle,* of Thomas Carlyle's *The French Revolution,* of Asa Gray's *Manual of Botany.*

The language of reports is also the mainstay of distinguished and memorable writers. It is the indestructible foundation of imaginative literature and, because it represents that which is real, is what makes for the sanity of true literature. English poetry abounds in examples. One thinks of Chaucer and Shakespeare and Milton. In addition, one remembers that it is this language of the concrete that so distinguishes, that is the very bread of the best English and American prose writers. Spontaneously there come to mind writers as distant in time and place as Robert Burton and Henry Thoreau. It is the language of much of *The Anatomy of Melancholy* and is what makes that book so richly human and so readable; it is the language of *Walden* and is what makes that book so real and health-giving. The style of these works is all substance, whole worlds are duplicated in their language, a language as bright and shining almost as the particulars it stands for.

II

Language itself is to a great extent responsible for the thoughts we have about phenomena of the world. The interpretation of facts and events and objects is built-in to the language, and from apples to Zouaves, we tend to see things and to understand ideas in the light of what has been said about them. The study of language consists, in part at least, in investigating the way in which language *makes* our world, past, present, and future.

We may call the language which makes our world the language of truths. The language of truths is the language of concepts and beliefs, of theories and opinions, of judgments and evaluations, of definitions, of systematic discourse, of explanation. It is the language in which ideas are expressed. It is the language of intellect. It is the language we use when we talk about the "meaning of life"; it is the language we use to "explain" a pattern of realities and to rationalize human experience. It is the vehicle for social beliefs and for precepts of conduct. It is the language of metaphysics, of moral philosophy, of esthetics, of education, of theology, of political and social theory, sometimes of the exact sciences.

The language of truths is a highly abstract language, and this makes it difficult, so that understanding of it, communication in it, calls for minds trained in its use. The language of truths is the language we use to present those vast generalizations that are based on a multitude of unspoken facts and details; and we have, as it were, to earn the right through knowledge of these facts and details to use this language. It is the language of Aristotle's *Politics*, of the *Summa Theologica*, of the *Discourse on Method*, of *An Essay Concerning Human Understanding*, of *The Critique of Pure Reason*, of John Stuart Mill, of Hegel, of John Dewey, of William James and Sigmund Freud.

The language of truths makes statements about reality, statements we often accept uncritically as part of our given body of knowledge, statements we often learn by heart as a part of our intellectual heritage. Innumerable are the *truths* in the history of human thought, many of them conflicting. We can only marvel at the resilience of the human mind that it can and does sort and sift them and try them out, preserving some, rejecting others. There were the truths of the ancient East, of the Mediterranean civilizations, of the European Middle Ages, of the modern West. Some we still cherish, some we have abandoned. The masters of abstract thought weigh their words with care and try to see life steadily and to see it whole. But in the end it is up to us, the readers and listeners, not to just one of us but to many of us, to decide whether a truth shall be respected, whether we find a truth to coincide with reality, whether a truth is good for all humanity.

The language of moral philosophy is the language of truths in its most compressed, aphoristic form, wisdom condensed into a few richly laden abstractions. Of all the many examples one might think of, none serve better to illustrate this language at its most concentrated than those celebrated sayings of the oracle

135

of Apollo at Delphi, "Know thyself" and "Nothing too much." Add to these the words of Periander, "Think as a mortal," and we have, in the pursuit of the good life, the abiding truths of Hellenism and of the humanism of the West. As Plutarch said, numberless are the philosophical discussions that have sprung from each as from a seed. Conveyed in one way or another over and over again in the writings of humane thinkers, these truths have become bright jewels in the crown of human wisdom.

III

There is another language which we may call the language of the arts. It is in some respects a perfect combination of the language of reports and the language of truths. It is the language of imaginative literature. It is the language of the prophetic writings of religion. It is the language of poetry. It is the language of Homer and Plato and Aeschylus and the King James Bible, and of Dante and Shakespeare and Milton and Keats, of Whitman, Tolstoi and Goethe, of Chekhov, Proust and James Joyce, of the poetry of Yeats and of T. S. Eliot. In its effect it goes beyond representation or duplication; it is not about something. It has its own life, its own being, its own permanence and perfection. Some miracle of transformation gives this language a will of its own. Some magic transforms mere words into living creations. It is, as has been said before, the language of the gods.

The direct approach to facts, which is the language of reports, contains a minimum of figurative language, since its purpose is contact with that which exists in the world. The formation of statements about reality, which is the language of truths, though often depending upon analogy, is cautious in the deliberate use of metaphor. But the language of the arts uses all the resources of symbolism and is particularly abundant of metaphorical expression. As objects and events are the substance of the language of reports, and as ideas are the substance of the language of truths, so relationships appear to be the substance of the language of the arts. It is the discovery of new and unsuspected relationships that constitutes the creative in all the arts. It is the composer's arrangement of different sounds into

136

an organic pattern that creates music, the painter's arrangement of different colors and shapes into an organic design that creates a painting, and so on. Similarly, it is the arrangement of the relationships of different realities and the relationship of different truths that is the language of poetry.

When King Richard (in Shakespeare's *King Richard II*), realizing that all is lost and that Bolingbroke is victor, says,

>   of comfort no man speak;
> Let's talk of graves, of worms and epitaphs;
> Make dust our paper and with rainy eyes
> Write sorrow on the bosom of the earth,

we are moved precisely because these dissimilars (tears are not rain, dust is not paper, the earth is not a bosom) are brought together into a unified pattern at once powerful in its appeal to our imagination and striking in appeal to our intellect because of that coalition of unlike objects and events and ideas, that extraordinary creation of orderliness, of unity, that arises out of the demonstrated relationship of bright particulars. When we wish to speak of our *being* in the world, when we wish to utter what we have felt in moments of deepest insight, when we bring to the surface those thoughts which really occupy us most, thoughts of our existence and of our relationship to heaven and earth, we use the language of the arts.

IV

It is possible, after all, that something more than language, or the symbolism of the arts, is required for total meaning. Language can go only so far; and beyond language, beyond meaning is existence—silence. True, we strive for total meaning through style, subject, context, relationships, and it may well be that in our most inspired moments we come close to total meaning. It may also be said that in this striving, there is more in the device of metaphor than meaning, meaning as we understand it in the linguistic and semantic sense. There comes to mind the poem "Ars Poetica" by Archibald MacLeish in which there are the lines, "A poem should not mean / But be." This suggests that there may be in the arts some insights that are more than the sum of the rhetorical devices used to convey them, something

137

beyond metaphor whose meaning is solely the creation of the original, of the singular, of the one. Let us pursue this thought a little further.

Out of all the facts of experience has come the most useful of ideas: the many. And by a miraculous effort of human thought has come the most profound of ideas: the one. There are two words "day," and one always means the same thing and the other never means the same thing. There is *today* with all its importunate particulars, and there are the days on the calendar, past and to come. The days, as we call them, follow in strict repetition, and out of all the days comes time. The content of the days may be different, but the days as units of time are the same, the useful, dependable same.

No two moments are alike, but time is eternally time. There is a strict frequency to the units of time, and each is like the other, but the composition of the moment is original. Listen to the opening measures of Beethoven's Symphony No. 4 and you will hear time captured and possessed in a unique pattern.

No two movements are alike, and yet there is all movement. The dancer never repeats herself, yet the figure is repeated many times. The areas that enclose objects or events are different, but space is eternally space, marked off into parcels, possessed and defined in architecture, painting, and sculpture.

All days look alike from a distance, as do the roses on the rose bush. People are repeated many times over, but the person next to me is different from all the others. There are many, but there is also the one. The many are alike, *en masse,* but the one, solo, is different. Art seeks to inform and express the one; art selects the event and makes it single and extraordinary.

The purpose of the language of the arts is justice. Language is in itself the request to be listened to. All thought comes finally to rest in the right to be heard, to put one's self on record, or, better, the right to exist, which is the right to be heard. Since, when examined by myself, I am what I am, I cannot help insisting upon that justice which was promised together with my individuality. Art is a plea for the practice of this justice, the articulation of the unique. The high purpose of art and religion is to keep us from despairing of that justice, which, as I say, accompanies by fiat my individuality. Or, to put it another way, if by chance justice does not exist, neither does individuality. The combined writings of Plato are the most eloquent plea yet fashioned for this justice, that it exist in the universe as an imperative, an absolute feature of being, which is my due by virtue of my existence.

Though present in most literature of the West, this cry for justice is more noticeable in the modern than in the older literature, that is, more is made of it, it becomes a central theme. If the old masters took their existence and originality for granted and chose mainly to examine themselves, to scrutinize their behavior, to see what was going on and what constituted their uniqueness (as in a self-portrait by Rembrandt, or in Hamlet's soliloquies, or in the foppish behavior of Etherege's Man of Mode), modern writers and artists seek to establish identity first, as though that were enough, since (which may be true) theirs—or the life of their characters—is now threatened with irreplaceable loss of identity.

Franz Kafka's *The Trial* and *The Castle* seem to me expressions, agonized and prolonged, of this modern plea for the justice of identity. Indeed, many modern works of distinction may be read in this fashion, which is revealing of the anxiety we all feel for our being, our individuality and the justice which is our due. This, at any rate, is the way I read the beautiful letters of Simone Weil in her *Waiting for God;* this is the meaning, or at least one meaning, of the character of Winston Smith in Orwell's *Nineteen Eighty-Four,* who holds out as long as he can against anonymity; this is why Saul Bellow's *Herzog* has been called "one long eloquent kvetch"; and this is the story that is being told by Humbert Humbert in Nabokov's *Lolita,* the story of *his* life, the plea for justice, or at least the right to be heard. Even J. Alfred Prufrock, in his way, is begging for that attention which will make him a little less likely to drown in the sea of human voices.

In the fine arts, numerous modern works utter this same anguished cry — "It is I." In the figures of the sculptor Alberto Giacometti one may read an existential anxiety of estrangement. In his bronze called "Man Pointing," the figure identifies and defines a new space, the inner psychic space of solitude. Here the figure is, perhaps, beseeching someone. It is as though he were being stared at by mute judges, the tension of his being in space heightened by the motionless gaze of his accusers. With a little effort of the imagination, one could fancy that the shapes in Picasso's painting entitled *Three Musicians* are the judges before whom this anonymous man is being examined. Here the judges do not appear as we would expect a camera to find them in a courtroom. Instead, they too inhabit a mysterious world of two dimensions, wearing masks and veils, clad as harlequins, monks, musicians. They are more than musicians. They are the ritual of a dream, an inquisition, a fantasy of judges. Chirico's dream figures, Giacometti's lonely strangers, Picasso's ceremonial judges are, we could say, illustrations for the novels of Franz Kafka. They live in a world enclosed by psychological fences, preternaturally still, expectant, silently facing anonymity.

We might talk about justice in still another way. If justice does not exist, we must create it. Now as we have seen, since art deals with the one, and since the one demands justice, then art is the way of being heard, of creating justice, of insisting upon singularity, of presenting the case for each of us. And that is the purpose of the arts, to present the case, to tell how it is with separate human beings. Language and symbols are the instruments with which this is accomplished. When language came into being so also did justice and individuality and art.

Curiously, one way of presenting the inimitable is through drawing attention to the likeness which it bears to something else. The similes in Homer are as important for the differences they imply as for the likenesses they state. Though he sometimes behaves like an animal, man is *not* an ox or a dog. Though the characters in the *Iliad* are on occasions (in some respect) like something otherwise quite different from them, it is, paradoxically, this likeness that gives them their individuality. Though man is related to animals, insects, even the winds and waters, he is different. There are many warriors but only one Diomedes, Tydeus' son; and the cry of each of these heroes is for justice, to tell how it was with him as *different* from the others. Homer does well by them all.

140

The men and women of the *Iliad* are a part of the rhythm and texture of all life. Again and again Homer brings forward one of the characters from out the ranks of the battle scenes and puts him in the center of the action against a background of all nature, reminding the reader in simile after simile that the hero is not unlike the nature around him, the horses, rivers, forests, lions, insects. Again and again Homer retires the various persons of the epic to their place among the many, where they are part of the whole, part of the mountains, plains, rivers, cities, boats, and sea. The one and the many make the pattern, as one image with another makes the design and tells the story on the shield of Achilleus.

The armies of the Greeks look like a forest fire

> along the crests of a mountain, and the flare shows far off,
> so as they marched, from the magnificent bronze the gleam went
> dazzling all about through the upper air to the heaven. (2,1.456)[1]

Powerful Agamemnon "with eyes and head like Zeus who delights in thunder" is

> like Ares for girth, and with the chest of Poseidon;
> like some ox of the herd pre-eminent among the others,
> a bull, who stands conspicuous in the huddling cattle;
> such was the son of Atreus as Zeus made him that day,
> conspicuous among men, and foremost among the fighters.
> (2, 1.479)

As the tribes pour from the ships to the plain of Skamandros, they are like

> the multitudinous nations of birds winged,
> of geese, and of cranes, and of swans long-throated
> in the Asian meadow beside the Kaystrian waters
> this way and that way make their flights in the pride of their
> wings, then
> settle in clashing swarms and the whole meadow echoes with
> them. (2, 1.459)

When Simoeisios fell "beneath the spear of high-hearted Aias," he dropped to the ground

---

[1]All quotations are from *The Iliad of Homer*, translated by Richmond Lattimore, The University of Chicago Press (Phoenix Books), Chicago, 1961.

> in the dust, like some black poplar,
> which in the land low-lying about a great marsh grows
> smooth trimmed yet with branches growing at the uttermost
>   tree-top:
> one whom a man, a maker of chariots, fells with the shining
> iron, to bend it into a wheel for a fine-wrought chariot,
> and the tree lies hardening by the banks of a river. (4, 1.482)

Is it not extraordinary that only by seeing likenesses do we see the unexampled? It is because Simoeisios is not a tree, nor a tree Simoeisios, that the comparison is so telling.

Hektor ranges in the foremost ranks of battle

> As when some hunting hound in the speed of his feet pursuing
> a wild boar or a lion snaps from behind at his quarters
> or flanks, but watches for the beast to turn upon him, so Hektor
> followed close on the heels of the flowing-haired Achaians.
> (8, 1.338)

The warriors take their position "in the blossoming meadow of Skamandros,"

> thousands of them, as leaves and flowers appear in their season.
> (2,1.468)

They are like

>   the multitudinous nations of swarming insects
> who drive hither and thither about the stalls of the sheepfold
> in the season of spring when the milk splashes in the milk pails:
> in such numbers the flowing-haired Achaians stood up
> through the plain against the Trojans, hearts burning to break
> them. (2,1.469)

Achilleus rises against Aineias like a lion,

> the baleful beast, when men have been straining to kill him,
>   the county
> all in the hunt, and he at the first pays them no attention
> but goes his way, only when someone of the impetuous young
>   men
> has hit him with the spear he whirls, jaws open, over his teeth
>   foam
> breaks out, in the depth of his chest the powerful heart groans.
>   (20, 1.165)

The figures of speech in the *Iliad* draw attention to the similarities between men and gods, men and insects, men and lions, men and horses, between men and fire, winds, plants, and water. The armies of the Greeks swarm like insects; the winds "fight" it out with each other; fire obliterates, as does war; as the lion

142

leaps on the neck of the ox, so Diomedes breaks the neck of his Trojan enemy; water can be angry and destructive; the drooping head of a dying warrior resembles the garden poppy bending beneath the weight of its yield; Paris in shining armor and laughing aloud moves through Troy like a stallion free of his stall who gallops over the plain in the pride of his strength; and terrible is the likeness of Helen's face to immortal goddesses.

In the age of the heroes, just as men and gods are closely related in the universe, so men and animals are related, and men and gods and nature. But each comes forward in proud singularity. All are parts of the whole, distinct but similar, unique but alike—one world of gods, men, beasts, plants, insects, natural forces. Yet in the dawn of the West, all objects stand out clearly against the horizon. The purpose of art (or at least one purpose) has not changed since the making of the *Iliad*. Against the background of the many, there is only one Ma Parker, however much she may resemble other women who are old and abandoned; there is only one George F. Babbitt, though he is very much like all the other Babbitts; there is only one Hurstwood among all the derelicts and castaways; only one Huckleberry Finn among all boys who have to make decisions beyond their years. There is but one Anna Karenina among all the suicides, but one Vautrin among thieves; only one Beatrice among all the choirs of the heavenly host, one Hektor though he tosses his son about in his arms and kisses him like any father, only one Helen of Troy. Each asks for justice, for integrity, and the literary artist responds, creating the portrait of the one against the background of many.

Before he dies, Hamlet, demanding that justice which is his due, cries out to Horatio:

If thou didst ever hold me in thy heart,
Absent thee from felicity awhile,
And in this harsh world draw thy breath in pain,
To tell my story.

The guiding, prevailing, master metaphor of the western tradition centers upon the idea of the one, the one who is *like* the many, but different. This intuition matures beyond its metaphor to meaning alone, limpid, palpable meaning. "The rest is silence."

Bibliographical Notes

(Many of the titles in these notes are available in paperback editions. In a few instances where it seemed appropriately informative, the paperback edition is especially noted. Otherwise, places and dates of publication are for those editions (whether in soft or hard cover) used by the author in connection with the text of this book.)

Introduction

For an analysis of schematic, symbolic, and tropic "fictions," see Hans Vaihinger, *The Philosophy of "As If"* (London, 1949). Vaihinger's work is a painstaking study of the assumptions implicit in metaphorical expressions. The propagandistic use of the ant metaphor is vividly described by a character in the novel *Arrival and Departure* by Arthur Koestler (New York, 1943). In the enthusiasm with which Koestler's Nazi speak, we see that the language he uses has convinced him beyond any doubt of the desirability of understanding that for political purposes, ants and men are identical. Talking about a "possible" future event will in itself tend to bring the event to pass. And the evidence selected to anticipate the event will direct the event to take the form foreseen. That people often behave according to the way they have expressed their expectations is discussed by Robert K. Merton in his article "The Self-Fulfilling Prophecy," in the *Antioch Review*, VIII (1948). For a brief comment on futuristic political theory, see also "The Vocabulary of Political Theory" by Weller Embler in *The Christian Scholar*, XLIX, 1, Spring, 1966. Though first published in 1941, *Language in Thought and Action* (2nd Edition, Paperback, New York, 1964) by S. I. Hayakawa is still a widely used textbook and one of the best introductions to General Semantics. It is based on the seminal work, *Science and Sanity* (1933; 4th Edition, 1958) by Alfred Korzybski and explores the relationships between language, thought, and behavior. The investigations of modern anthropology have been richly rewarding in showing the association of language and culture. "The General Theory of Magical Language" by Bronislaw Malinowski is an early and penetrating study of linguistic-cultural interdependence. This essay, which appeared originally in *Coral Gardens and Their Magic* (1935), is reprinted under the title "The Language of Magic" in *The Importance of Language* ed. by Max Black (Englewood Cliffs, New Jersey, 1962). In any study of the influence of language on human behavior, one must inevitably be indebted to the work of Benjamin Lee Whorf. Selected writings of Benjamin Lee Whorf are available in *Language, Thought, and Reality,* ed. by John B. Carroll (Cambridge, Massachusetts, 1956; Paperback Edition, 1964). *Permanence and Change* by Kenneth Burke (New York, 1935) was the book which most influenced my first thoughts about metaphor and meaning. It is still a stimulating work and has recently been published in a Paperback Edition (Indianapolis, 1965).

Literature as Metaphor

There are few books or articles which deal directly with the subject of this chapter, that many works of literature and the fine arts are extended metaphors of the inner life. The following are, however, pertinent. *Permanence and Change* (listed in the bibliographical note for the Introduction) by Kenneth Burke is rich in ideas; and his *Attitudes Toward History* (first published in two volumes in 1937) is particularly rewarding for the development of his theory of the symbolic action of literature. The observations on Aubrey Beardsley and Oscar Wilde were inspired by the chapter entitled "The Tragic Generation" in *Trembling of the Veil* (1922) by William Butler Yeats. The reference to the Impressionist painters derives in part from Oscar Wilde's essay "The Decay of Lying" (from *Intentions*, 1891); the idea of the fair and shining appearance is from Nietzsche's *The Birth of Tragedy*. In general, however, the point of view taken in this chapter is cultural and psychological; inevitably *The Decline of the West* (One Volume Edition, New York, 1939) by Oswald Spengler will be responsible for studies of the cultural meaning in metaphor, and the works of Sigmund Freud for the psychological. Freud's *Collected Papers* are a storehouse of insights and suggestions for further study. *Psychoanalysis & American Literary Criticism* (Detroit, 1960) by Louis Fraiberg is thorough and dependable scholarship. Especially provocative is his chapter "Hanns Sachs: The Creative Act," in which he discusses Sachs' theory of art as the formalizing of fantasy. *Pseudonyms of Christ in the Modern Novel* (Pittsburgh, 1962) by Edwin M. Moseley is an illuminating and perceptive study of the sacrificial hero in fiction, the modern substitute for the Christian archetype. *Music as Metaphor* (Minneapolis, 1960) by Donald N. Ferguson is a pioneer work, thoughtful and valuable in its analysis of the expressive qualities of music. Mostly, however, it is the imaginative literature itself that one turns to for enlightenment and understanding of the strategical use of literature as surrogate for inner human feelings. The novels and stories of Joseph Conrad are highly susceptible to this interpretation of the art of fiction. Most of the writings of Franz Kafka (all allegorical literature, in fact) may be read as objectified substitutes for the inner life, as may also some of the stories of Thomas Mann (e.g., "Mario and the Magician"). As an example for further study, consider the stories of Edgar Allan Poe. In *The Cask of Amontillado* the alter ego walls up the *other* self, the alcoholic self, as punishment for self-murder. The narrator watches himself, as it were, is present at his own disintegration, and the story becomes a fantasy substitute for the violent conflict in the author's own mind.

Design as Metaphor

Any approach to modern design must take seriously into account the research and critical opinions of Lewis Mumford. Of his many distinguished works, I am most indebted in this chapter to his collection of articles entitled *From the Ground Up* (New York, 1956). *Pioneers of Modern Design* (New York, 1949) by Nikolaus Pevsner is a dependable and discerning study of design in crafts, architecture, painting, interior furnishings from William Morris to Walter Gropius. The many publications of the Museum of Modern Art, on bridges, architecture, modern painting, sculpture, industrial design are useful and valuable reference works. *The New Vision* (1928) by L. Moholy-Nagy is a signifi-

146

cant book in the history of modern design. "A Study In Architectural Semantics" by Katherine Gilbert (re-printed in *Architecture in America,* edited by William A. Coles and Henry Hope Reed, Jr., New York, 1961) is an important investigation into the language used to talk about architecture. Both sensitive and learned, *Styles in Painting* (New York, 1963) by Paul Zucker is rewarding for layman and scholar. *Rococo to Cubism in Art & Literature* (New York, 1960) by Wylie Sypher is a penetrating discussion of the philosophic backgrounds of styles in art and literature from the eighteenth century to the present. The most valuable single work, the major inspiration for this chapter, is *Space, Time and Architecture* (Cambridge, 1942) by Siegfried Giedion. It could be said of Giedion as he himself said of Jakob Burckhardt that he shows a period in its entirety, "with regard not only for its painting, sculpture and architecture but for the social institutions of its daily life as well."

Metaphor in Everyday Speech

Though much of the content of this chapter was gathered from empirical observation of everyday usage, the following works on language have contributed to the shaping of the thoughts here. For its development in the context of modern cultural linguistics, the subject of meaning in the everyday speech of a people must inevitably draw upon the seminal work of Benjamin Lee Whorf. (See the bibliographical note for the Introduction.) So, too, one will find important to his thoughts on communication the early and still valuable research of I. A. Richards, not only *The Meaning of Meaning* (1923) by C. K. Ogden and I. A. Richards, but *Practical Criticism* (1929) by I. A. Richards. For wide-ranging studies of cultural meaning in communication, the two books, *Language, Meaning and Maturity* (New York, 1954) and *Our Language and Our World* (New York, 1959), both made up articles which first appeared in *ETC.: A Review of General Semantics* and edited by S. I. Hayakawa, are stimulating and readable. *The Tyranny of Words* (New York, 1938) by Stuart Chase was one of the first books to call our attention to the importance of understanding that words often use *us,* instead or our using *them.* Another arresting study of the relationship of language to behavior is *Signs, Language, and Behavior* (New York, 1946) by Charles Morris. Though not as pertinent to this chapter, *The Human Use of Human Beings* (Garden City, New York, 1954) by Norbert Wiener is important in any study of modern theories of communication, especially of communication and education, since, according to Wiener, "Cybernetics takes the view that the structure of the machine or of the organism is an index of the performance that may be expected from it." *Language: An Inquiry Into Its Meaning and Function* (New York, 1957) edited by Ruth Nanda Anshen is an opulent collection of essays by such distinguished authors as W. H. Auden, George Boas, Erich Fromm, Charles W. Morris, Paul Tillich, Huntington Cairns, who write on such subjects as the language of poetry, of history, of dreams, of mysticism, of theology, of jurisprudence. *The Wonder of Words* (1938; republished, New York, 1957) by Isaac Goldberg is a neglected masterpiece. For many years I have found it a treasury of humanistic learning in the history of language and its relationship to culture. Lastly, although the book was published some years after this chapter was written, a reference here to *Understanding Media: The Extensions of Man* (New York, 1965) by Marshall McLuhan is distinctly called for. *Understanding Media* is a work of extraordinary originality and of major importance in the study of information theory and modern media of communication. Written in a style as speedy and affluent as the culture it talks about, the book is abundant of McLuhan's own use of analogy and metaphorical expression drawn from the machinery of the "electric age," and as provoking of thought as the analogies that inform Spengler's *Decline of the West*. Interestingly, what *Understanding Media* has to say appeals spontaneously and with ready acceptance to many of its student readers, as, being a college teacher, I can attest. This is perhaps because it says, among other things, that they (anyone and everyone) are on an equal footing, when it comes to modern media of communication, with the most learned college professor. All watch the same movies, the same television shows, listen to the same radio broadcasts, read the same newspapers, etc., even if they do not, in private, read the same books.

Symbols in Literature and Art

Modern psychology has inspired much of the literature on symbolism in the arts, and one thinks immediately of the *Complete Psychological Works of Sigmund Freud,* beginning, obviously enough, with the masterwork, *The Interpretation of Dreams* (1900). Together with the writings of Freud, and probably for the creative writer and artist as influential, the works of Carl Gustav Jung are clearly indicated. *Modern Man in Search of a Soul* (New York, 1933) contains *passim* the Jungian theory of archetypes, unconscious primordial images which play so large a part in artistic communication. Anthropology, too, has contributed richly to studies in symbolism, and *The Golden Bough* (1 Volume, Abridged Edition, New York, 1942) by Sir James George Frazer is still a treasury of ideas and a seminal work for its influence on artist and critic. Though not always specifically related to the thoughts expressed in this chapter, the following items have been among the more significant readings relevant to the essay. *The Heritage of Symbolism* (London, 1943) by C. M. Bowra; *The Meeting of East and West* (New York, 1946) by F.S.C. Northrop, especially the chapter on "The Rich Culture of Mexico"; "The Unconscious Element in Literature and Philosophy" in *The Unwritten Philosophy and Other Essays* (Cambridge, England, 1950) by F. M. Cornford (edited with an Introductory Memoir by W. K. C. Guthrie); *Axel's Castle* (New York, 1936) by Edmund Wilson; *Art Now* (New York, 1936) by Herbert Read; and of especial value *Studies of Type-Images in Poetry, Religion and Philosophy* (London, 1951) by Maud Bodkin. I am most indebted, however, to *The Lost Language of Symbolism,* 2 volumes, (London, 1912; 1951) by Harold Bayley, a historical rather than a psychological study, reliable, scholarly, endlessly fascinating "enquiry into the origin of certain letters, words, names, fairy-tales, folklore and mythologies."

Five Metaphors from the Modern Repertory

Doubtless there are innumerable works which deal with the prison as an institution of man from time immemorial; as a subject in the history of literature and art, however, I know of none.

The idea of incarceration, of the soul, for instance, as being *in* the body, is indeed early in the Near-Eastern and Mediterranean civilizations. (See Spengler's *Decline of the West*, Volume Two, Problems of the Arabian Culture, Chapter VIII, "The Magian Soul.") The metaphor of the descent into Hell is also of ancient origin, and of course the most artistic and profound representation of this inner experience is Dante's *Divine Comedy*. The metaphor of the journey, and indeed of the whole idea of the purgatorial pilgrimage through life, is discussed with rare sensitivity and learning in *Dante's Drama of the Mind, A Modern Reading of the Purgatorio* (Princeton, 1953) by Francis Fergusson. For the wasteland metaphor there is the invaluable *From Ritual to Romance* (Garden City, New York, 1957) by Jessie L. Weston. This book is by now so well known to students of the poetry of T. S. Eliot that it scarcely needs to be mentioned here; but it is the constantly rewarding work of a fine scholar. For an understanding of the Renaissance image of man, I have found *The Dignity of Man* (Cambridge, 1947) by Herschel Baker to be both scholarly and readable. *New Images of Man* (New York, 1959) by Peter Selz is a perceptive study of one aspect of contemporary art. Though not related specifically to the metaphor of the machine, *The Education of Henry Adams* (New York, 1931) is still one of the most penetrating studies of the subtle emotional and intellectual effects of the change to the machine culture of the modern world. Psychological and metaphysical sickness is the subject of a very great deal of contemporary literature and art; one is tempted to say, the leading subject. Again, the works of Sigmund Freud are indicated. His *The Problem of Anxiety* (New York, 1936; translated from the German by Henry Alden Bunker) is a major work and explains with customary ingenuity and insight the relation between behavior (as symptomatic) and anxiety. First published more than half a century ago, *The Varieties of Religious Experience* by William James is a classic in its field and promises to remain so for a long time to come. The chapters on "The Religion of Healthy-Mindedness," "The Sick Soul," and "The Divided Self" are especially apropos. "Art and Neurosis" (in *The Liberal Imagination*, New York, 1953) by Lionel Trilling is illuminating.

150

"Of the artist," Trilling points out, "we must say that whatever elements of neurosis he has in common with his fellow mortals, the one part of him that is healthy, by any conceivable definition of health, is that which gives him the power to conceive, to plan, to work, and to bring his work to a conclusion." The theme of "Philoctetes: The Wound and the Bow" (in *The Wound and the Bow*, New York 1947) by Edmund Wilson is that though sick, the artist serves humanity. Philoctetes, "the victim of a malodorous disease which renders him abhorrent to society and periodically degrades him and makes him helpless, is also the master of a superhuman art which everybody has to respect and which the normal man finds he needs." *Two Legends: Oedipus and Theseus* (New York, 1950, translated from the French by John Russell) by Andre Gide contains modern recastings of the ancient stories. The comparison of the "healthy" man-of-action with the maimed seer is rendered with the usual Gidean brilliance. To the several metaphors mentioned in the last pages of this chapter, two should be added. Though examples are not many — or perhaps one should say not easily recognized — the figure of the "whirlpool" of life is entering the modern repertory. This is not the image of the Baroque vortex, which had a lifelike character, as of growing plants, vines, leaves in organic profusion, but rather is, as Loren Eiseley uses it in *The Firmament of Time* (New York, 1962) "a vast black whirlpool spinning faster and faster, consuming flesh, stones, soil, minerals, sucking down the lightning, wrenching power from the atom, until the ancient sounds of nature are drowned in the cacophony of something which is no longer nature, something instead which is loose and knocking at the world's heart, something demonic and no longer planned — escaped, it may be — spewed out of nature, contending in a final giant's game against its master." (Pgs. 123,4.) The metaphor (if it is a metaphor) of life-as-a-game deserves considerable examination, especially in the light of the use of the metaphor by writers who value the consciousness-expanding qualities of the drug LSD. All departments of life may now be talked about in terms of the game and its rules — the game of sex, the game of politics, of having fun, of playing the role of teacher, doctor, lawyer, engineer, salesman, etc., in appropriate situations. Release from the narrow restraints of the game is discussed by Richard P. Marsh in "Meaning and the Mind-Drugs" in *ETC.: A Review of General Semantics*, XXII, No. 4, December, 1965. The use of the metaphor of the "game" is essential, it seems, in talking about the psychedelic drug, as though its qualities are what they are *because* life in society in the twentieth century is a game.

The Language of Criticism

Before the advent of modern academic criticism, the critics were mostly the professional and creative writers. (One remembers without hesitation such names as Sainte-Beuve, Coleridge, Ruskin, Arnold, Taine, Bruntiere, Robert Schumann, Hector Berlioz, Henry James, Baudelaire, James Huneker, George Bernard Shaw, Thomas Mann, Paul Valery.) Now, however, from the American universities there is an unremitting flow of critical literature, a large body of which is literary scholarship and appears in the learned journals. There are, at the same time, a number of first-rate contemporary critics who reside on American campuses. With few exceptions these writers and editors are learned, their style urbane, their taste impeccable.

One thing is certain, however. Aside from academic literary scholarship, where all writings are potential grist to the mill, taste in the enjoyment of criticism is almost exclusively and unaccountably one's own. A critic speaks to us or he does not; we like what he says and the way he says it, or we dislike what he says and the way he says it, or we are indifferent. In addition to authors mentioned in the text of this chapter and to those listed in the notes above, the following modern writers are to me rewarding reading and were, one way or another over a period of time, inspirations in preparing for this essay. Henry James (see, for example, his *French Poets and Novelists*, New York, 1964); George Bernard Shaw (see *Shaw on Music*, A selection from the Music Criticism of Bernard Shaw made by Eric Bentley, Garden City, New York, 1955); Benedetto Croce (see his *European Literature of the Nineteenth Century*, London, 1925); Van Wyck Brooks; I. A. Richards; T. S. Eliot; Lionel Trilling; Allen Tate; Lionello Venturi (see his *Modern Painters*, New York,

1947); Francis Fergusson (see his *The Idea of A Theatre,* Princeton, 1949); Joseph Wood Krutch; Herbert Read (see, for example, his "Surrealism and the Romantic Principle," 1936); Andre Malraux (especially *The Voices of Silence,* translated from the French by Stuart Gilbert, New York, 1953); Edmund Wilson; Virginia Woolf; Katherine Anne Porter (see her *The Days Before,* New York, 1952). Invaluable as a reference work on the various schools and methods of modern criticism, *The Armed Vision* (New York, 1955) by Stanley Edgar Hyman is systematic, learned, intellectually discriminating.

The Rhetoric of the Absurd

It is to the literature of Existentialism that one quite naturally turns in his study of the philosophy of the Absurd in contemporary creative works. With reference to this chapter, see *The Myth of Sisyphus and Other Essays* (translated by Justin O'Brien, New York, 1955) by Albert Camus; and for a critical analysis of Camus' novel *The Stranger,* see Sartre's essay, "Camus' The Outsider," in *Jean-Paul Sartre Literary and Philosophical Essays* (translated from the French by Annette Michelson, New York, 1962). *The Challenge of Existentialism* (Bloomington, Indiana, 1955) by John Wild and *Irrational Man: A Study in Existential Philosophy* (New York, 1958) by William Barrett are excellent critiques. *Existential Psychology* (edited by Rollo May, New York, 1961) is a brief but valuable introduction to the subject; and A. H. Maslow's paper, "Existential Psychology — What's In It for Us?" is relevant to one of the themes of this chapter. "The loss of illusions," says Maslow, "and the discovery of identity, though painful at first, can be ultimately exhilarating and strengthening." *The Courage To Be* (New Haven, 1957) by Paul Tillich is richly rewarding in its representation of the need for courage in the face of the loss of meaning in the modern world. Tillich's description of Luther's courage in spite of the negativity of the sixteenth century enlarges our understanding of what is meant by the courage to *be*: "It has been rightly said that Albrecht Durer's engraving, 'Knight, Death, and the Devil,' is a classic expression of the spirit of the Lutheran Reformation and — it might be added — of Luther's courage of confidence, of

153

his form of the courage to be. A knight is riding through a valley, accompanied by the figure of death on one side, the devil on the other. Fearlessly, concentrated, confident he looks ahead. He is alone but he is not lonely. In his solitude he participates in the power which gives him the courage to affirm himself in spite of the presence of the negativities of existence." *The Mystery of Being* (Volume I, *Reflection & Mystery,* Chicago, 1950) by Gabriel Marcel ranges meditatively over evidences of the personal and spiritual disintegration of modern man. Gertrude Stein's lecture "Composition as Explanation" (see *Selected Writings of Gertrude Stein,* edited by Carl Van Vechten, New York, 1946) anticipates the Absurd in literature and art, as does also her *Four Saints in Three Acts.* Things are not what they seem or even what they are said, from moment to moment, to be; and composition is "a using everything a beginning again and again and then everything being alike then everything very simply everything . . . [is] naturally simply different." *The Dada Painters and Poets* (edited by Robert Motherwell, New York, 1951) is a bountiful and valuable collection of materials from the Dada movement. *The Theater of the Absurd* (Garden City, New York, 1961) by Martin Esslin is a helpful study. Opening in New York, December 27, 1965, *The Persecution and Assassination of Jean-Paul Marat As Performed by the Inmates of the Asylum of Charenton Under the Direction of The Marquis de Sade* by Peter Weiss (paperback edition, New York, 1966) is a stunning work of the contemporary theatre and may be discussed as a dramatic study of history itself as Absurd, the event a brief moment full of sound and fury which trails off into sleep and nothingness. There is a long essay entitled "History as a System" (in *Toward a Philosophy of History,* New York, 1941) by the Spanish philosopher Jose Ortega y Gasset which I have long admired and in which I find an early existential reading of the idea of history. In several ways, indirect, to be sure, but related, this essay of Ortega's can serve as collateral reading in the attempt to understand what it is that Peter Weiss expresses with such inspired dramatic power in *Marat/Sade.*

Language and Truth

Since this chapter is more in the "familiar" form and makes no pretense at offering a systematic study of language *or* truth, it is perhaps better in the bibliographical note to list only those few titles and authors which I am confident were influential, in one way or another and over the years, in shaping my thoughts and feelings about the idea of "truth." Mostly my truth and my language are in the American traditions of Pragmatism and Idealism. For instance, there is the essay *Nature* (1836) by Ralph Waldo Emerson, and there is *Walden* by Henry David Thoreau, in which New England pragmatism and New England transcendentalism are combined. Walt Whitman was on the side of both truth and language, and his *Democratic Vistas* is a sturdy combination of self-reliance and social responsibility. *Varieties of Religious Experience* by William James is steadfastly rewarding, as vital today in its humanism as it was when the chapters were delivered as the Gifford Lectures in Edinburgh in 1901-1902. Historical truth as Henry Adams saw it with massive erudition and a New England background, and literary truth as Henry James saw it with artistic sensitivity and a New England background are expressed in the acute observations of *The Education of Henry Adams* and in the novels and essays of Henry James. As American pragmatic truth and in characteristically American language, too, the works of Mark Twain, William Dean Howells, Hamlin Garland, Francis Parkman (see, for example, *The Oregon Trail*), Edgar Lee Masters, and Robert Frost are in the tradition of practical idealism. The American naturalists are refreshing in the candid way in which they see the world of nature. The writings of John Burroughs (for example, *Indoor Studies*, Boston, 1900, and *Under the Maples*, Boston, 1921) are abundant of open-eyed observations of the facts of nature. Among the modern humanists devoted to the American traditions are Van Wyck Brooks and Joseph Wood Krutch. (See, for instance, Krutch's *The Desert Year*, New York, 1952). The expression of truth in the language of architecture may be found in the designs and writings of Louis Sullivan (for a recent biography, see *Louis Sullivan, An Architect in American Thought* by Sherman Paul, Englewood Cliffs, N. Y., 1962); the expression

155

of truth in the language of music may be found in the compositions of Charles Ives (see his *Essays Before A Sonata,* edited by Howard Boatwright, New York, 1962); and the expression of truth in the language of the visual arts may be found in the paintings and watercolors of Winslow Homer, in which one sees the return to sources, to first things, to the elemental, pragmatic, unavoidable truth rendered with extraordinary visual power.

Metaphor and Beyond

For parts I and II of this chapter, I am indebted to *Language in Thought and Action* by S. I. Hayakawa (see bibliographical notes for the Introduction) for his exposition of "the language of reports" and the "language of social control" which I have called (as perhaps suiting a little better my purpose here) the language of truths. Parts I and II are offered mainly as a background for the thoughts in the rest of the essay, which are designed to express somewhat the difference between language as a vehicle for exposition and language as a medium for literature. The wonder of language is that it can do so many things so supremely well; the wonder is that the instrument can be so supple and yet so strong. Still, as T. S. Eliot says in the poem "Burnt Norton" (from *Four Quartets,* New York, 1943), even words sometimes "strain" and "break" under the burden of too much meaning. That is what is meant by "Beyond" in the title of this chapter. After all is *said,* there remains only the experience of meaning; and as students of mysticism have often pointed out, one can report the most profound meanings, the ecstatic visions, only haltingly, at best, and in fragments. There may well be more than one way of "knowing." Ours is for the most part the practical way of what we call scientific knowledge; and it is self-evident that this knowledge is of enormous value in our daily lives. But as Henri Bergson says in his *An Introduction to Metaphysics* (translated by T. E. Hulme, New York, 1949), there are "two profoundly different ways of knowing a thing. The first implies that we move round the object; the second that we enter into it. The first depends on the point of view at which we are placed and on the symbols by which we express ourselves. The second neither depends on a point of view nor relies on any symbol." An arresting account of Bergson's philosophy is to be found in *The Misuse of Mind* (New York, 1922) by Karin Stephen. In *Mysticism* (New York, 1955) by Evelyn Underhill, one reads: "There is no certitude to equal the mystic's certitude: no impotence more complete than that which falls on those who try to communicate it. . . . Nevertheless, the greater part of mystical literature is concerned with the attempts of the mystics to share their discoveries." And so it is also with the creative writer. He uses all the subtle devices of rhetoric, all the techniques of literary art and of symbolism, to give him power to tell his story. In Marcel Proust's rendering of the evanescent impressions of the sensory life into a flowing consciousness of the hawthorn blossoms in the chapter "Combray" in *Swann's Way* (translated by C. K. Scott Moncrieff, New York, 1928), he uses all the splendors of language. As the hawthorn hedge heaps flower upon flower, so Proust adds metaphor to metaphor in a profusion of radiant images — of flamboyant churches, of music, of altars adorned, of the sea, of cups of pink marble, of confections, of masterpieces of painting — that express the Bergsonian intuition of duration in terms of the unfolding realization in time of beauty itself.

Index

Absurd, philosophy of, 95, 97, 98n, 108, 116, 95-116 *et. passim*

Adams, Henry, 113; *Mont-Saint-Michel and Chartres*, 83f, 83n; *The Education of Henry Adams*, 69f, 83n, 150, 155

Addams, Charles, 8

Aeschylus, 136; *Eumenides*, 115; *Oresteia*, 115f

Ain, Gregory, 25

Anderson, Maxwell, *Winterset*, 21

Anshen, Ruth Nanda, "Language as Communication," 39n; ed., *Language: An inquiry Into Its Meaning and Function*, 148

Architecture, vii; architectural design, 21-24

Aristotle, 86; *Poetics*, 91f, 100, 110; *Rhetoric*, 111n; *Politics*, 135

Armitage, Kenneth, 67

Arnold, Matthew, "Who Prop, Thou Ask'st, in These Bad Days, My Mind?," 13, 152

Arthurian legends, 64

Auden, W. H., 55; "In Memory of W. B. Yeats," 60n; 113

Baker, Dorothy, *Young Man With a Horn*, iv

Baker, Herschel, *The Dignity of Man*, 150

Barr, Alfred H., Jr., *A Brief Guide to the Exhibition of Fantastic Art, Dada, Surrealism*, 99

Barrett, William, *Irrational Man: A Study in Existential Philosophy*, 153

Baskin, Leonard, 68

Baudelaire, Charles, "Anywhere Out of the World," 72; "Reversibility," 72; 72n, 152

Bayley, Harold, *The Lost Language of Symbolism*, 149

Baziotes, William, 56

Beardsley, Aubrey, 3, 90, 145

Becker, Carl L., *Freedom and Responsibility in the American Way of Life*, 37n

Beckett, Samuel, *Endgame*, 68n, 111f; *Waiting for Godot*, 104

Beethoven, L. v., *Fidelio*, 59; *Symphony No. 6*, 84; *Symphony No. 4*, 138

Behaviorism, 43

Bentley, Eric, *The Playwright as Thinker*, 88, 88n

Beowulf, 110

Berg, Alban, *Wozzeck*, 5

Bergson, Henri, *An Introduction to Metaphysics*, 156f

Berlioz, Hector, "Beethoven's *Sixth Symphony*," 84f, 152

Berman, Eugene, 52

Bernstein, Joseph, M., ed. *Baudelaire, Rimbaud, Verlaine, Selected Verse and Prose Poems*, 72n; 73

Bible, King James, 112, 136

Blackmur, R. P., "Unappeasable and Peregrine," 86, 86n; "W. B. Yeats: Between Myth and Philosophy," 87, 87n
Blake, William, 59
Bodkin, Maud, *Studies of Type-Images in Poetry, Religion, and Philosophy,* 149
Bonaparte, Napoleon, 69
Bonnard, Pierre, 17f
Botticelli, Sandro, 54, 120f
Bowra, C. M., *The Heritage of Symbolism,* 149
Breton, Andre, 7
Breuer, Marcel, 25
Bridges, design of, 20f
Brooks, Van Wyck, 152, 155
Bruntiere, Ferdinand, 152
Burchfield, Charles, 52
Burckhardt, Jakob, 147
Burke, Kenneth, 86; *Permanence and Change,* 87, 87n, 145; *Attitudes Toward History,* 145
Burns, Robert, 130; "Tam o' Shanter," 100
Burns, Robert K., *Yearbook of the American Iron and Steel Institute,* 71n
Burroughs, John, 126; *Indoor Studies,* 155; *Under the Maples,* 155
Burton, Robert, *The Anatomy of Melancholy,* 134
Butler, Reg, 67
Byron, George Gordon, Lord Byron, viii; 59

Cain, James M., 8
Camus, Albert, *The Fall,* 30n; *The Plague,* 75n; *The Stranger,* 75, 103; *The Rebel,* 96, 108; *The Myth of Sisyphus and Other Essays,* 153
Canterbury Tales, The, 64, 101
Capek, Karel, *R.U.R.,* 70, 101
Capote, Truman, *The Grass Harp,* 53
Carlyle, Thomas, *The French Revolution,* 134
Cezanne, Paul, 26, 54
Chagall, Marc, 95
Chaplin, Charles, *Modern Times,* 69, 70, 101
Chase, Stuart, *The Tyranny of Words,* 147
Chaucer, Geoffrey, 82, 100, 134
Chekhov, Anton, 136
Chesterfield, Earl of (Philip Dormer Stanhope), 15, 17
Chirico, Giorgio de, 6; *Il Trovatore,* 12ff; 140
Churches, design of, 21f
Clouet, Jean, *Diane de Poitiers,* 52
Clurman, Harold, "Introduction" to *Seven Plays of the Modern Theatre,* 102
Cocteau, Jean, 7
Communication, viii, 117-132 *et. passim*
Coleridge, Samuel Taylor, 92, 152
Conrad, Joseph, *Heart of Darkness,* 1f; 146
Cooke, Rose Terry, *Steadfast,* 121
Cornford, F. M., *The Unwritten Philosophy and Other Essays,* 149
Crane, Hart, 7, 21

Criticism, 93f; 80-94 *et. passim*
Critique of Pure Reason, 135
Croce, Benedetto, *European Literature of the Nineteenth Century,* 152
Cubism, 22f, 55, 96
Cybernetics, ix

Dada Painters and Poets, The, 154
Dali, Salvador, 6, 7
Dante, 61, 112, 136; *Inferno,* 110; *Divine Comedy,* 150
Darwin, Charles, *The Voyage of the Beagle,* 134
Debussy, Claude, 4, 89f; *Afternoon of a Faun,* 90
Delphic oracle, sayings of, 136
Descartes, Rene, 108; *Discourse on Method,* 135
Design, 14ff; modern, 22f; philosophy of, 25
Dewey, John, 135
Dickens, Charles, 69, 103
Dickinson, Emily, 1
Disney, Walt, 100n
Dostoevsky, F. M., *Notes from Underground,* 76
Doughty, Charles M., *Travels in Arabia Deserta,* 134
Dubuffet, Jean, *Woman with Furs,* 67
Dufy, Raoul, *Open Window in Nice,* 17
Dumas, Alexandre, *The Count of Monte Cristo,* 59
Durer, Albrecht, "Knight, Death, and the Devil," 153

Eames, Charles, 25
Eiseley, Loren, *The Firmament of Time,* 151
Eliot, George, 103, 132
Eliot, T. S., 86, 136, 152; *The Waste Land,* 7, 60, 63f, 69; *The Cocktail Party,* 9; "The Hollow Men," 14; "The Love Song of J. Alfred Prufrock," 73; *Four Quartets,* 73, 86; *The Family Reunion,* 88; "Hamlet," 92; "Burnt Norton," 130, 131
Ellis, Havelock, 69
Embler, Weller, "The Vocabulary of Political Theory," 144
Emerson, Ralph Waldo, 122; *Nature,* 155
Empson, William, 86
Epictetus, 13
Ernst, Max, 6
Essay Concerning Human Understanding, 135
Esslin, Martin, *The Theatre of the Absurd,* 154
Etherege, Sir George, 139
Existentialism, 42, 61f, 74, 76, 124
Expressionism, 5
Eyck, Jan van, *Arnolfini Portrait,* 52

Faulkner, William, *Sanctuary,* 7, 8 10; "A Guest's Impression of New England," 122f
Ferguson, Donald N., *Music as Metaphor,* 146
Fergusson, Francis, *Dante's Drama of the Mind, A Modern Reading of the Purgatorio,* 150; *The Idea of a Theatre,* 153

Fitzgerald, F. Scott, 7; *The Great Gatsby*, 64f
Forster, E. M., "What I Believe," 129
Fraiberg, Louis, *Psychoanalysis & American Literary Criticism*, 146
France, Anatole, 92; "The Disputes of the Flute Players," 81n
Frazer, Sir James, 9; *The Golden Bough*, 149
Freud, Sigmund, 31, 42, 71, 135; *Collected Papers*, 145f; *Complete Works*, 149; *The Interpretation of Dreams*, 149; *The Problem of Anxiety*, 150
Friedrich, Caspar David, 52
Frost, Robert, viii, 7, 61n, 155, "Mowing," 121

Garland, Hamlin, 155
Gauguin, Paul, 54
Genet, Jean, *The Balcony*, 99n, 101f
Genteel Tradition, 15-19
Giacometti, Alberto, "Man Pointing," 139f
Gide, Andre, *Two Legends: Oedipus and Theseus*, 151
Giedion, Siegfried, *Space, Time, and Architecture*, 147
Gilbert, Katherine, "A Study in Architectural Semantics," 147
Gilman, Lawrence, *Orchestral Music: An Armchair Guide*, 85n
Ginsberg, Allan, *Howl*, 76
Goethe, Johann Wolfgang von, 28, 112, 136
Gogh, Vincent van, 5, 54
Goldberg, Isaac, *The Wonder of Words*, 148
Goya, Francisco, *Don Manuel Osorio*, 54
Graces, The (classical mythology), 17
Gray, Asa, *Manual of Botany*, 118, 134
Greene, Graham, 8
Grieg, Edvard, viii
Gropius, Walter, 24

Hammett, Dashiel, 8
Hardy, Thomas, 103; "Hap," 76, 107
Hawthorne, Nathaniel, 100
Hayakawa, S. I., *Language in Thought and Action*, 144, 156; ed. *Language, Meaning and Maturity*, 147; ed. *Our Language and Our World*, 147
Hegel, G. W. F., 135
Hemingway, Ernest, *The Sun Also Rises*, 7; "The Killers," 9f
Hersey, John, 61n
Hess, Thomas B., 68, 68n
Hicks, Edward, *The Peaceable Kingdom*, 54
Hitchcock, Alfred, 8
Hodeir, Andre, *Since Debussy: A View of Contemporary Music*, 108n
Holbein, Hans, 52
Homer, v, vi, 13, 14, 101, 136; *Odyssey*, 97; *Iliad*, 1, 126, 140-143
Hopper, Edward, 7, 51, 52
Housman, A. E., 114, 115, 130
Howells, William Dean, 155
Hugo, Victor, *Les Miserables*, 59
Huneker, James, 89; *Promenades of an Impressionist*, 93; 93n, 152

Huxley, Aldous, "Sir Christopher Wren," 81f, 82n
Huysmans, J. K., 90
Hyman, Stanley Edgar, *The Armed Vision,* 153

Ibsen, Henrik, *Ghosts,* 88
Impressionism, 4f, 51, 89f
Ionesco, Eugene, *Rhinoceros,* 101
Ives, Charles, *Essays Before A Sonata,* 156

Jackson, Charles, *The Lost Weekend,* 114f
James, Henry, 16, 77; *The Ambassadors,* 16f; *Portrait of a Lady,* 127;
    French Poets and Novelists, 152
James, William, 135; *The Varieties of Religious Experience,* 150, 155
Johnson, Philip C., 25
Joyce, James, 136
Jung, Carl Gustav, 53; *Modern Man in Search of a Soul,* 149

Kafka, Franz, 61n, 63n, 105, 140, 146; *Metamorphosis,* 5, 65f, 67, 97, 101;
    "Notes from the Year 1920," 60n, 62f; "The Burrow," 66; *The Castle,*
    104, 139; *The Trial,* 104, 139
Kaufmann, Walter, *The Faith of a Heretic,* 62n
Keats, John, 50, 136; "Ode to a Nightingale," 52
Kierkegaard, Soren, 62n
Kline, Franz, 56
Kline, Morris, *Mathematics in Western Culture,* 80n
Koestler, Arthur, *Arrival and Departure,* 144
Kokoschka, Oskar, 5
Kooning, Willem de, 67f
Korzybski, Alfred, *Science and Sanity,* 144
Krutch, Joseph Wood, 153; *The Desert Year,* 155

Language, of reports, 133f; of truths, 134-136; of the arts, 136-138
Lattimore, Richmond, trans., *The Iliad of Homer,* 141n
Lawrence, D. H., *Lady Chatterly's Lover,* 7
Leger, Fernand, 56
Lewis, C. Day, *A Hope for Poetry,* 113
Lewis, C. S., *Surprised by Joy,* 27
Lewisohn, Ludwig, ed. *A Modern Book of Criticism,* 81n
Lowell, James Russell, 19

MacLeish, Archibald, "Ars Poetica," 137
McIntire, Samuel, 19
McLuhan, Marshall, *Understanding Media: The Extensions of Man,* 148
Maillart, Robert, 20f
Malinowski, Bronislaw, "The General Theory of Magical Language," 145
Mallarme, Stephane, 4
Malory, Sir Thomas, *Le Morte D'Arthur,* 46-48
Malraux, Andre, *The Voices of Silence,* 153

Mann, Thomas, 97; *The Magic Mountain,* 75n; "Mario and the Magician,"
146, 152
Marcel, Gabriel, *The Mystery of Being,* Vol. I, 154
Marsh, Richard P., "Meaning and the Mind-Drugs," 152
Marvell, Andrew, 78
Marx, Karl, *Capital,* 69
Masaccio, 54
Maslow, A. H., "Existential Psychology — What's In It for Us," 153
Masters, Edgar Lee, 155
Matisse, Henri, 17f, 52
May, Rollo, ed. *Existential Psychology,* 153
Mendelsohn, Eric, 25
Menotti, Carlo, 8
Merton, Robert K., "The Self-Fulfilling Prophecy," 144
Metaphor, iv-ix *et. passim;* 43, 58, 136f, 140-143; the novel as, 1-11 *et. passim;* design as, 12-26 *et. passim;* in everyday speech, 27-44 *et. passim*
Meyerbeer, Giacomo, 81
Michelangelo, Buonarroti, 67
Mielziner, Jo, 21
Mill, John Stuart, 135
Miller, Arthur, 8; *Death of a Salesman,* 10f
Milton, John, 104, 112, 134, 136; *Paradise Lost,* 27; *Lycidas,* 130f
Moholy-Nagy, L., *The New Vision,* 146
Mondrian, Piet, 56; *Victory Boogie-Woogie,* vii
Monet, Claude, 4, 26
Moreau, Gustave, "Salome," 90
Morris, Charles, *Signs, Language, and Behavior,* 148
Morris, George L. K., "What Abstract Art Means to Me," 55
Moseley, Edwin M., *Pseudonyms of Christ in the Modern Novel,* 146
Motherwell, Robert, 56
Mumford, Lewis, *From the Ground Up,* 146
Munch, Edward, 52

Nabokov, Vladimir, *Lolita,* 108, 139
Neutra, Richard, 25
Nietzsche, Friedrich, 4, 31, *The Birth of Tragedy,* 145
Northrop, F. S. C., *The Meeting of East and West,* 149

O'Connor, Flannery, *Wise Blood,* 98f; "Good Country People," 108f
O'Neill, Eugene, 31; *The Hairy Ape,* 66n; *Dynamo,* 69f; *Mourning Becomes Electra,* 88
Ortega, y Gasset, Jose, 127; *The Dehumanization of Art,* 54; "History as a System," 154
Orwell, George, *Animal Farm,* 66, 66n; *Nineteen Eighty-Four,* 131f, 139
Osborne, John, *Look Back in Anger,* 39
Osler, Sir William, *The Principles and Practice of Medicine,* 134
Owen, Wilfred, 107

Parkman, Francis, *The Oregon Trail,* 155
Paul, Sherman, *Louis Sullivan, An Architect in American Thought,* 155

Periander, 136
Pevsner, Nikolaus, *Pioneers of Modern Design*, 24, 146
Pharmacopoeia of the United States, 133
Phidias, v
Philipson, Morris, ed. *On Art and Artists* by Aldous Huxley, 82n
Picasso, Pablo, *Guernica*, 23; *Three Musicians*, 140
Piranesi, Giovanni Battista, 50, 59
Pissarro, Camille, 4
Plato, 136, 139, *Phaedo*, 58
Platonism, 4, 43
Plutarch, 136
Poe, Edgar Allan, "The Fall of the House of Usher," 51f; "The Cask of Amontillado," 146
Porter, Katherine Anne, *The Days Before*, 153
"Prisoner of Chillon," 62n
Proust, Marcel, 136; *Swann's Way*, 157

Rachmaninoff, Sergei, "Isle of the Dead," 90
Raphael, 67
Ravel, Maurice, 4
Read, Herbert, *Art Now*, 149; "Surrealism and the Romantic Principle," 153
Reed, Carol, 8
Rembrandt van Rijn, 118, 139
Richards, I. A., 152; *Practical Criticism*, 88, 147; *The Meaning of Meaning* (with C. K. Ogden), 147
Rilke, Rainer Maria, *Rodin*, 92f
Rimbaud, Arthur, 96
Robert, Hubert, 51
Robinson Crusoe, 46
Robinson, Edwin Arlington, 7
Roebling, John and Washington, 21
Romney, George, 17
Rosenberg, Harold, 55f
Rosenfeld, Paul, "Debussy," 89, 90n
Rossellini, Roberto, 8
Roszak, Theodore, *Iron Throat*, 76n
Ruskin, John, 152

Saint John the Divine, *Revelation of*, 111
Sainte-Beuve, C. A., 152
Sandburg, Carl, 7
Saroyan, William, 7
Sartre, Jean-Paul, 7, 61n; *Nausea*, 69, 74f, 74n, 103; *No Exit*, 61f; *Jean-Paul Sartre Literary and Philosophical Essays*, 153
Schelling, Friedrich von, vii
Schonberg, Arnold, *Pierrot Lunaire*, 5
Schumann, Robert, 152
Seligmann, Kurt, 6; "Balcony I," 99n
Selz, Peter, *New Images of Man*, 67f, 76n, 150

Shakespeare, William, 67, 143, 136; *Anthony and Cleopatra*, 110; *Hamlet*, 38, 71, 139, 143; *King Richard II*, 137; *King Henry IV*, Part I, 109f; *King Henry V*, 78; *Macbeth*, v, 101; *Othello*, vii, 53; *The Tempest*, 100, 125

Shaw, George Bernard, 82; *The Quintessence of Ibsenism*, 88; *Shaw on Music*, 152

Shelley, Mary, *Frankenstein*, 70

Shostakovich, Dmitri, viii

Signs, 46

Sir Gawain and the Green Knight, 64, 100

Sisley, Alfred, 4

Socrates, viii, 58

Sophocles, 13, 14

Spender, Stephen, 113; *World Within World*, 113

Spengler, Oswald, *The Decline of the West*, 145, 148, 150

Spillane, Mickey, 8

Spingarn, J. E., "The New Criticism," 93

Stein, Gertrude, 75, 130; "Composition as Explanation," 154; *Four Saints in Three Acts*, 154

Steinbeck, John, 7; "The Leader of the People," vf; *Sea of Cortez*, vi

Stella, Joseph, 21

Stephen, Karin, *The Misuse of Mind*, 157

Stoker, Bram, *Dracula*, 101, 101n

Stravinsky, Igor, 7; *L'Histoire du Soldat*, 5

Summa Theologica, 135

Surrealism, 6, 99

Sweeney, James Johnson, vii

Swift, Jonathan, 66, 100, 111; *Gulliver's Travels*, 34f

Symbols, 46-48

Sypher, Wylie, *Rococo to Cubism in Art & Literature*, 147

Taine, Hippolyte, 152

Tanguy, Ives, 6

Tate, Allen, 152

Tchelitchew, Pavel, 7

Tennyson, Alfred Lord, vi; "Locksley Hall," 81

Thackery, William Makepeace, 103

Thoreau, Henry David, 19f, 123; *Walden*, 134, 155

Through the Looking Glass (Lewis Carroll), 45

Tillich, Paul, 68; *The Courage to Be*, 153

Tinguely, Jean, 71

Tolstoi, Leo, 136

Tree of Life, 20, 24, 52f

Trilling, Lionel, 152; "Art and Neurosis," 150

Twain, Mark, 155

Tzara, Tristan, "Lecture on Dada," 96

Underhill, Evelyn, *Mysticism*, 157

Vaihinger, Hans, *The Philosophy of "As If,"* 144
Valery, Paul, 152
Van der Rohe, Mies, 25
Velazquez, Diego, 54
Venturi, Lionello, *Modern Painters,* 152
Vitruvius, *Ten Books on Architecture,* 49f

Wagner, Richard, 81, 111n
Wain, John, "Along the Tightrope," 42
Walsh, Raoul, 8
Warren, Austin (with Rene Wellek), *Theory of Literature,* 92, 92n
Webern, Anton, 107f
Webster, Daniel, 69
Weil, Simone, "Spiritual Autobiography," 63n; *The Need for Roots,* 32; *Waiting for God,* 76f, 139
Weiss, Peter, *The Persecution and Assassination of Jean-Paul Marat as Performed by the Inmates of the Asylum of Charenton Under the Direction of The Marquis de Sade,* 154
Wellek, Rene (with Austin Warren), *Theory of Literature,* 92, 92n
Weston, Jessie L., *From Ritual to Romance,* 150
Whitman, Walt, 136; *Democratic Vistas,* 155; *Leaves of Grass,* 91; "Out of the Cradle Endlessly Rocking," 91
Whorf, Benjamin Lee, *Language, Thought, and Reality,* 145, 147
Wiener, Norbert, *The Human Use of Human Beings,* ix, 148
Wild, John, *The Challenge of Existentialism,* 153
Wilde, Oscar, 26; *Salome,* 2f, 4, 90; "The Decay of Lying," 145
Wilder, Billy, 8
Williams, Tennessee, 8; *A Streetcar Named Desire,* 73; *Period of Adjustment,* 73f
Wilson, Edmund, 153; *Axel's Castle,* 149; "Philoctetes: The Wound and the Bow," 151
Wolfe, Thomas, 7
Woolf, Virginia, 153
Wood, Grant, 7
Wordsworth, William, vi, 75; "Nuns Fret Not At Their Convent's Narrow Room," 62n; "Ode on the Intimations of Immortality," 59f
Wright, Frank Lloyd, 23
Wyeth, Andrew, 52

Yeats, William Butler, 3, 76, 136; "A Prayer for My Daughter," 32; *Trembling of the Veil,* 145

Zucker, Paul, *Styles in Painting,* 147

University
of Windsor

Date Due

APR 13 2009
RETURNED